NAMING
AND BLESSING

NAMING
AND BLESSING

A Book of Name Prayers

Andrew Tawn

Illustrations by Pat Schaverien

Souvenir Press

CONTENTS

Foreword by Lord David Hope vii

Introduction by the Author ix

Author's Note xi

Name Prayers A–Z 2

Appendix with shortened names and variant spellings.............227

Complete Index of all Name Prayers 271

FOREWORD

One of the fascinating and intriguing facts of our times is that quite a number of surveys over the last few years have indicated that in spite of the decline of what may be termed 'institutional' religion and consequently church attendances, people nevertheless seem to be no less enthusiastic for what is called 'spirituality'.

Of course 'spirituality' covers a wide range both of meaning and of practice and can be applied to any religious faith or none. Further, people say that they are 'spiritual' but not religious; that they pray but they do not go to church. And such sentiments are confirmed by the number and range of books on almost every aspect of spirituality from tree hugging and crystal gazing to contemplation and worship.

Almost every Minister, of whatever denomination, will testify to the fact that 'occasional' services such as baptisms, weddings, funerals, confirmations, memorial services and the like – all these draw in quite large numbers of people who would themselves claim only to be 'occasional' attenders and yet who are open and responsive to what the service has to offer in terms of its prayer and worship. Further 'Abide with me', 'Jerusalem' and other such popular hymns, even when sung on the football pitch are a sign that there yet remains something innately religious deep within the human person, and rather after St Augustine – 'our hearts are restless until they rest in Thee'.

The genius of this book of acrostic prayers is that Andrew Tawn, whilst in no way compromising the Christian tradition – rather the more confirming it – has nevertheless produced a collection of prayers which can be used so very easily and readily by a much wider range of people than simply the committed Christian. They will undoubtedly resonate with and be both appreciated and used by those for example who bring their children for baptism – but will also appeal to a much wider range of people both young and old. Parents considering a possible name or names for a child will find here as well an invaluable resource.

Furthermore for those who may have lost either the will or the way to pray, these prayers will surely introduce afresh churchgoer and non churchgoer alike to the language of prayer and blessing – and not least to the wonder, love and care of the God and Father of Our Lord Jesus Christ.

Throughout the Scriptures names almost invariably have a special meaning – they establish our identity and tell us who we are. Right at the very beginning Abram is told 'your name will be Abraham, for I have made you the ancestor of a multitude of nations'; the prophet Hosea names his successive children Jezreel, Lo-ruhamah, and Lo-ammi – all of them signs of the rejection of the people and of the destruction which was to come upon them because of their unfaithfulness. But above all there is the name of Jesus – Emmanuel – God with us for ever and always – a name invoked by millions of people day by day and in every situation and circumstance. It is the name which is above every name – the name at which every knee is to bow – a name which brings forgiveness, reconciliation and peace.

This collection of prayers will surely be invaluable to ministers of every kind who officiate at all manner of services and in many different settings. They will also open up for everyone a very simple and practical, but none the less profound, way of prayer in which each person will surely come to discover a special, personal and unique blessing; an endorsement of who and what they are as a beloved child of God.

✝ David

Rt Revd and Rt Hon Lord Hope of Thornes KCVO.

INTRODUCTION

I invite you to use this book for every time in life when names are important.

It is for prospective parents as they choose the names for their son or daughter with love and care, and then it is to help them pray for their children as they grow.

It is for ministers wishing to add a personal touch to baptisms, confirmations or weddings.

It is for all who want to pray by name for others and ask God's blessing upon them.

It is for the times when we wish the very best for someone but cannot find the words.

Perhaps it may also be for the times when we feel the need of God's blessing upon our own name.

Our names play a significant role in religious practices. In the baptism service a child is named before God. In marriage the bride and groom join their names together in their vows. For thousands of years people have prayed by name for those they are concerned about and most churches include in their public intercessions the names of those who are sick or suffering.

In the Bible a person's name is very often connected to their personality, essence and true nature. The name Adam means 'human being' but is derived from *adama*, the Hebrew word for 'earth' from which Adam was formed. Jesus re-names Simon as Peter, which means 'rock', knowing that he would become the rock on which the early church was built.

It is also in this sense that we pray to God, 'Hallowed by thy name' and we 'call upon the name of the Lord' (Acts 2.21) when we need his help. God knows each one of us individually as a good shepherd who 'calls his own sheep by name' (John 10.3). And when God says, 'I have called you by your name, you are mine'

(Isaiah 43.1) he is saying that he knows us intimately – not only the name our parents gave us, but who we are inside.

These prayers began with my nephew Dylan's naming ceremony. All the guests were invited to bring a poem or picture to go in an album as a memento of the day. The fact it was a *naming* ceremony gave me the idea of writing an acrostic prayer on the letters of Dylan's name. Later it occurred to me that this was something I could do for the children I baptised at my church. Soon I was getting requests from my congregation for prayers for their children, or parents, or friends and this book began to take shape.

Many of the prayers weave in the meaning of the name or a Bible verse which suggested itself to me as I was writing. Some paraphrase other famous prayers or carry echoes of well-known hymns. Some simply play upon the sound of the name.

There are so many names it was hard to know where to stop. In the end this was decided for me by the deadline for publication and the limits of space. I am sorry if a name you are looking for is not here. Perhaps I will continue to write more. But if this book inspires others to write their own name prayers that would be even better.

Above all I hope and pray that those who read these prayers will rediscover the significance of their names and the names of those they care about, and may know the touch of God's blessing upon them.

May God bless you,

Andrew Tawn
Addingham 2010

AUTHOR'S NOTE

This book is not meant to be read from cover to cover. Rather you are invited either to scan the book for the names you are looking for or else browse in a more leisurely way and let the prayers recall to you the people you know who bear these names.

All names are arranged in alphabetical order with each name preceded by a brief explanation of its meaning. Where a name has shortened forms or alternative spellings you will find the variations in the appendix and this is marked throughout the text. So, for instance, Alexander and Alastair appear in the main text but Alexa, Alexis, Alexandra, Alasdair and Alistair will be found in the appendix. For easy reference please refer to a complete index at the back of the book where all names are listed alphabetically.

All Biblical quotations are from The Revised Standard Version. Bible references also are taken from the RSV but should apply to all other versions of the Bible. In some Bibles, such as the Authorized Version, the spellings of names may differ slightly but the author has endeavoured to use the most popular spellings for the prayers in this collection.

To all those for whom these prayers were originally
written and most especially for Helen,
Rosemary and Lucy.

NAME PRAYERS
A–Z

Aaron (m) is the brother of Moses in the Bible. The name may originate from the Egyptian language (Aaron was born in slavery in Egypt) or from Hebrew, and is thought to mean 'bright' or 'high mountain'.

Above you, may God watch over you,

Ahead of you, may God lead you,

Round you, may God protect you,

On you and those you love, may God pour his blessings,

Near you always, may God keep you in his love.

Abigail (f) derives from the Hebrew *Abigayil* meaning 'Father's joy'. *Abba* was the Aramaic word Jesus used to address God as Father, or 'Daddy' (Mark 14.36). For Abbie and Abby (f) see appendix.

Abba, Father, bless you:

Bless you with joy in your sadness;

In your need, bless you with plenty.

God give you blessings of love in your friendships,

And blessings of faithfulness in your love;

In your working, blessings of fulfilment;

Let your whole life be blessed with peace.

Adam (m) is the first human being in the Bible (Genesis chapters 1–5). The name means 'human' and is derived from the Hebrew *adama* meaning 'earth'. God made *adam* from the *adama*. The story of God's creation of Adam is followed by Adam's temptation and fall – a reminder that to be tempted and sometimes to fail is part of the human condition.

Against all temptation, may God defend you;

During all trouble, may God support you;

After every fall, may God raise you;

May God who made you, bless you and keep you.

The name Addison (f/m) comes from a surname meaning 'Adam's son'. This prayer is based upon the Lord's Prayer (Matthew 6.9–13). *Abba* is the Aramaic word for 'Father' (Mark 14.36).

Abba, Father, bless you and give you

Daily forgiveness, daily bread,

Deliverance from evil;

In temptation may he give you

Strength to do his will

On earth, as it is in heaven,

Now and forever. Amen.

Adrian (m) comes from the Latin Hadrian meaning 'of Adria', a town in northern Italy. The third line refers to John 4.10 and the fourth and fifth lines echo Psalm 121.8.

Afresh each day, God give you his blessing,

Down to earth, God meet you each day,

Refreshing the soul, God give you living water,

In your going out, God send you in his service,

And in your coming in, God replenish you with peace,

Now and every day, God hold you in his love.

Agnes (f) comes from the Greek *hagnos* meaning 'pure'.

As deep as the deepest ocean,

Greater than the highest mountain,

Nearer than your innermost thought,

Eternal as the maker of time itself,

So may God's love for you be.

The name Aidan (m) or Aiden (m) derives from the Irish *Aodh*, a Celtic God of sun and fire. Aidan (died 651 AD) was one of the first and greatest leaders of the church in England. He was summoned by King Oswald from the monastery on the island of Iona and became Bishop of Lindisfarne, bringing Celtic Christianity to the north of England. For Aiden see appendix.

As the air you breathe, God fill you and inspire you,

In the water of life, God refresh you and cleanse you,

Dependable as the earth, God support you on your journey,

As the fire of love, God warm you and protect you,

Now may God bless you and always be with you.

———

Ailsa (f) is a Scottish name, derived from the small island called Ailsa Craig in the Firth of Clyde.

Almighty God keep Ailsa

In your loving care and protection,

Let your peace be ever within her,

Shine your light ever before her,

And may your blessing be ever upon her.

Alan (m) derives from the Celtic *alun* meaning 'concord'. For Allan (m) see appendix.

As night follows day,

Let the peace of God be upon your resting;

As day follows night,

New blessings from God be upon your rising.

Alastair (m) is the Scottish Gaelic form of Alexander. For the variant spellings Alasdair (m) and Alistair (m) see appendix.

As armour to the soldier,

Like a lighthouse to the sailor,

As the parachute to the pilot,

So may God be to you

To defend and deliver you.

As the lifeboat to the lost,

In the stormy sea, so may God

Rescue and restore you.

Albert (m) comes from the old German meaning 'noble' and 'bright'.

A blessing of God on your eyes;

Let them always see goodness and beauty.

Blessings of God on your hands;

Everything they touch be prosperous.

Rich blessings of God in your heart;

To keep you forever in his love.

Alexander (m), with its shortened version Alex (m/f), comes from the Greek meaning 'defender of men'. There are several names, both male and female, which derive from Alexander. For Alexandra (f), Alexa (f) and Alexis (f) see appendix.

As you turned your Son's death to new life,

Lord, turn Alexander's troubles to blessings,

Endings to beginnings,

e**X**change his sorrows for joys.

And as you promised

Never to forsake those who love you,

Defend Alexander against every danger,

Everywhere he goes, go with him,

Remain with him and bless him for ever.

As God turned his Son's death to new life,

Let him turn your sorrows to joys,

Endings to beginnings,

eXchange your troubles for blessings.

Alfie (m) is a shortened form of Alfred, which is derived either from Aelfraed meaning 'wise counsel' or from Ealdfrith, 'old peace'.

As high as the highest star you can see,

Longer than the days of your life,

Further than the furthest place you will go,

In depth deeper than the deepest sea,

Even so may God's love for you be.

Alice (f) comes from the German for 'noble woman'. Alicia, Alison, Allison, Alisha, and Alyssa (all f) come from Alice. Throughout the Bible clothing is used as a metaphor for the qualities of godliness. In the New Testament this metaphor extends to being clothed in Christ himself. These prayers draw on Isaiah 61.10, Proverbs 31.25, Galatians 3.27 and Ephesians 4.24. For Alicia, Allison and Alisha see appendix.

Adorn Alice,

Lord of all loveliness,

In robes of peace and love and joy,

Clothing her in the garment of salvation,

Enfolding her in your blessings.

Adorn Alison,

Lord of all loveliness,

In robes of righteousness and holiness;

Strength and dignity be her clothing;

On her shoulders place the garment of salvation,

None other than Jesus Christ himself.

Almighty God,

Let Alyssa be enfolded in your love,

Your peace and your joy;

Shield her in your cloak of protection;

Shelter her under the shadow of your wings;

And bless her always.

Amalie (f), like Amelia, derives from the German for 'labour'. This blessing is based on the Biblical prayer known as the Aaronic blessing (Numbers 6.22–27).

All the days of your life,

May God bless you, be gracious to you,

And give you peace.

Let the Lord make his face to shine upon you,

In all your ways watch over you,

Evermore look kindly on you.

Amanda (f) and the shortened version Mandy (f) come from the Latin meaning 'loveable'.

Always and everywhere

May God bless you

And keep you in his love,

Nurture in you a loving nature,

Develop in you a loveable disposition,

And delight in all that is lovely within you.

May you be blessed by God,

And your journey be guided by his light,

Needs be satisfied, your hurts be healed,

Difficulties overcome, your dreams fulfilled,

Your heart be filled with his love.

Amber (f) is named after the gemstone, formed from fossilized tree resin. The warm yellow colour of the gemstone is held to symbolise optimism and hope.

As resin, turned to amber, is precious in our eyes,

May Amber be precious in your sight, Lord:

Bless her with your grace and peace;

Embrace her in the warmth of your love;

Radiate upon her your light and your hope.

Amelia (f) derives from the German for 'labour'. For Amelie (f) see appendix.

All the days of your life,

May God bless you,

Encourage and equip you,

Lead and enlighten you,

Instruct and inspire you,

And accompany you always.

Amy (f) and Aimee (f) mean 'beloved', and come from the Latin *amare* (to love) via the French *aimer*.

Abundant Love, bless Amy your beloved,

Mighty Love, keep her from harm,

Yearning Love, seek her when she is lost.

At all times may God bless you,

In all places may God be with you,

May he enrich you with his joy,

Encircle you with his peace,

Embrace you with his love.

Andrew (m) comes from the Greek meaning 'manliness'. Andrew was one of Jesus' twelve disciples, the brother of Simon Peter. The last line of this prayer refers to Psalm 139.14. For Andrea (f) see appendix.

Around and within, the protection of God to you,

Now and forever, the blessing of God to you,

Deep and wide, the love of God for you,

Rewarding and challenging, the calling of God for you,

Everywhere and here, the presence of God with you,

Wonderful and fearful, the life of God within you.

Angela (f) derives from the Greek *angelos* which means simply 'a messenger.' An angel is a messenger from God. This prayer alludes to Hebrews 13.2 ('Do not neglect to show hospitality to strangers, for thereby some have entertained angels unawares' RSV), which itself refers to the story of Genesis 18.1–16. For Angel (m/f) and Angelina (f) see appendix.

As some have ministered to strangers,

Not knowing they were angels,

God send his angels to you.

Entertain them, serve them;

Let them minister to you

And through them may God bless you.

Angus (m) is an Anglicized version of the Gaelic name meaning 'excellent virtue', or 'one choice'.

All that is good,

Nourishing and needful,

Grant to Angus, generous God,

Upholding him in your love,

Shielding him with your strength.

Anna (f) and Ann (f) derive from the Hebrew for 'grace'. This prayer is based upon words from Romans 8.38–39. For Anne (f) and Annette (f) see appendix.

According to God's promises, and by his grace,

Neither death, nor life, nor things present, nor things to come–

Nothing in all creation can separate you from his love:

And so may God keep you in his love for ever.

Around and within, the protection of God to you,

New and old, the gifts of God to you,

Now and forever, the blessing of God to you.

Annabel (f) is a combination of Anna and *belle*, French for 'beautiful'.

Almighty Father, by your grace be

Near to Annabel to support and encourage her;

Never forsake her when she is

Afraid or in need;

Bless her and prosper

Everything she does, wherever she goes

Let your love and peace be with her.

Anthony (m) comes from the Roman family name Antonius. It has also been suggested that the name derives from *anthos*, Greek for 'flower'. For Antony, Anton, Antonio (all m) and Antonia (f) see appendix.

A blessing of life to you, first of all –

New life, life in all its fullness;

Then a blessing of peace to you –

Holy peace, which the world cannot give;

Over all, a blessing of love to you –

Never-ending, ever-hoping, all-enduring love,

Your heavenly father's love for you.

———

Archie (m) is a shorter form of Archibald, which came into use in England through the Norman conquest but comes originally from the Old German meaning 'bold' or 'brave'. This prayer takes its starting point from the architectural image of the arch.

Above you, the arch of God's love to protect you,

Rock beneath, the foundations of God to support you,

Crossing all dangers, the bridge of God to carry you,

Holding you firm, the pillars of God to strengthen you,

In your heart and soul, the peace of God to keep you,

Every day of your life, the blessing of God be upon you.

Ariana (f) derives from the Greek name Ariadne, which means 'very holy'. For Arianna (f) see appendix.

At each need a blessing from God:

Refreshment when you are weary,

In your trouble, God's peace,

After sadness, his comfort,

New hope after disappointment,

And after death, new life.

Arthur (m) comes either from the Gaelic meaning 'stone' or the Celtic for 'bear'. The third line refers to John 11.25.

Author of peace and love and joy,

Reside within you, restore you, bless you;

The risen Christ, the resurrection and the life,

Hold you, heal you, raise you;

Unseen Spirit, untamed power,

Renew you, revive you, rekindle you.

ASHLEY – *as a shaft of sun in a woodland clearing.*

Ashley (m/f) is derived from a place name meaning 'ash tree' and 'clearing' or 'wood'.

As a shaft of sun in a woodland clearing,

So may your love stream down on Ashley,

Heavenly Father, source of light.

Like the myriad stars in a clear night sky,

Even so send down on Ashley

Your countless blessings, Lord of life.

Ashton (m) comes from the place name meaning 'town of ash trees'.

All your life be full of God's blessings:

Spirit filled with peace,

Heart filled with love,

Thoughts filled with grace,

Opportunities filled with hope,

Now and each day filled with eternity.

Audrey (f) means 'noble strength' (from Old English). This prayer was inspired by an ancient prayer which begins with the words 'Prevent us' in the now almost forgotten sense of 'go before us': 'Prevent us, O Lord, in all our doings with thy most gracious favour' (from the Book of Common Prayer).

Anticipate all that Audrey needs, Lord,

Understand her thoughts before she forms them,

Direct her steps until she finds the path,

Rescue her before she meets the danger,

Embrace her before she even seeks your face,

Your gracious favour go before her always.

Austin (m) is a shortened form of Augustine, which means 'great' or 'august'. This prayer is based upon words of St. Augustine of Hippo (354–430 AD), one of the greatest theologians and spiritual writers of the Church.

Almighty God, our hearts are restless

Until they find their rest in you;

So may Austin know you and love you

That he may find true peace

In your presence, and in your love

New life and joy.

Ava (f) may either be a variant of Eve or possibly from the Latin for bird (*avis*).

All things vital and virtuous

Vouchsafe for Ava, O Lord,

And save her from vice and vanity.

Bailey (m/f) may come from the surname meaning 'bailiff', or from the fortification of a city or castle. For the female version please change the pronouns.

Be for Bailey a rock of refuge,

A fortress to defend him

In times of trouble and danger.

Let the walls of his castle keep evil without,

Even as its halls welcome within

Your love, your peace and your blessings.

Barbara (f) comes from the Greek meaning 'strange' or 'foreign'. The name is probably onomatopoeic, imitative of the sound of a foreign language.

Be for Barbara

A source of strength,

Renewal and inspiration,

Blessed Trinity,

Almighty Father,

Redeeming Son,

And Holy Spirit.

Barnaby (m) comes from Barnabas which means 'son of encouragement' in Aramaic. In the Bible Barnabas was one of St. Paul's companions. (Acts 4.36–7; 9.27; 11.22–24).

Bless Barnaby, Lord,

And bless his growing and learning;

Renew your blessings of love with each rising,

New blessings of peace with each resting;

And bless his giving and receiving,

Bless his crying and his laughing;

Your blessing be upon him forever.

Beatrice (f) means 'bringer of blessings' from the Latin *beatus* meaning 'blessed'. This prayer is based on Jesus' blessings known as the Beatitudes (Mt. 5.3–12 & Luke 6.20–23).

Blessings of God's mercy be upon you,

Even as you yourself are merciful;

And blessings of God to satisfy within you

The hunger and thirst for justice and truth;

Rich blessings when you are poor in spirit;

In your times of sadness, blessings of comfort;

Christ bless you with peace and love,

Even as you bring love and peace to others.

Belinda (f) is of uncertain origin but may be derived from the Italian *bella* meaning beautiful.

Bless Belinda with your beauty, Lord:

Enlighten her mind with your truth;

Let your love so dwell in her heart

It will shine through her words and her work;

Nurture in her your graceful bearing;

Decorate her spirit with jewels of joy;

And crown her being with peace.

Benjamin (m) comes from the Hebrew meaning 'son of the right hand' or 'favourite' (see Genesis 35.17–18). Benjamin was Jacob's youngest son, and the only full brother of Joseph (by Rachel, their mother). This prayer is based upon the list of the nine fruits of the Spirit in Paul's letter to the Galatians (5.22–23).

Bless Benjamin, Lord, with the seeds of your Spirit;

Encourage their rooting and growing within him;

Nurture them to bear good fruit:

Joy, peace, love in his heart;

And patience, faithfulness, self-control in his mind;

May he show kindness, gentleness, goodness

In the way he treats his neighbour and himself,

Now and always. Amen.

Ben (meaning in Hebrew 'Son') is a shortened form of Benjamin.

By your grace may Ben be blessed,

Encircled by your protection, Father,

Nourished by your love.

Bethany (f) is a Biblical place name (John 11.1), the home of Martha and Mary and their brother Lazarus whom Jesus raised from the dead.

Be for Bethany, Lord,

Easter after Lent,

The sunshine after rain,

Home after travel,

After illness, health,

New life even after death,

Your love even before her birth.

———

Beverley (f/m) comes from a place name meaning 'beaver stream'. For the male version please change the pronouns. For Beverly (f/m) see appendix.

Bestow your love on Beverley, Lord,

Every moment of every day;

Vouchsafe to keep her in your peace

Every day of every year;

Raise her up from every fall,

Lead and guard her on every path;

Every year of evermore,

Your blessing be upon her.

Blake (m) comes either from the Old English *blaec* meaning 'black' or from *blac* meaning 'white or pale'.

Between you and each person may there be peace,

Let God's love flow between you and each friend,

And between you and each sin may God set his mercy,

Keep his shield between you and each harm,

Establish his blessing between his heart and yours.

Bradley (m) comes from a surname and place name meaning 'broad clearing or wood'.

Bless Bradley, Lord,

Richly with your grace,

And bless him

Deeply with your peace.

Let your light shine upon him brightly

Every day of his life,

Your love keep him safely forever.

Brandon (m) may mean 'broom hill' or may be a variant of Brendan – Mount Brandon in Ireland is named after St. Brendan. St. Brendan (c.486 – c.575) was known as 'Brendan the navigator' because of his travelling and sea voyages.

By his grace, may God be your

Rudder in the swirling current,

Anchor in the running tide,

North pole for your compass,

Driving breeze for your sails,

Oars when you find yourself becalmed;

Near and far, your constant blessing.

Brenda (f) comes from the Norse meaning 'brand', 'torch' or 'sword'.

Burn, Holy Spirit,

Rekindle in Brenda the fire of your love;

Embrace her, Heavenly Father,

Nurture her as your own child;

Defend her, Risen Jesus,

And raise her with you to new life.

Brendan (m) comes from the Irish Gaelic meaning 'prince' (or possibly 'stinking hair'). St. Brendan (c.486 – c.575), an Irish monk and abbot, was known as 'Brendan the navigator' because of his travelling and sea voyages. St. Brendan's popularity owes much to a tenth century romance chronicling his quest for an island of promise in the Atlantic ocean.

Blessings of God on your going out;

Returning, God bless your coming in.

Every voyage you make be

Navigated by his guidance;

During every storm may he protect you

And bring you safely home to harbour.

Near and far, God be with you always.

The name Brian (m) derives from the Irish Gaelic for 'strength' or 'power'. For Bryan (m) and Brianna (f) see appendix.

Be your strength drawn from the power of God,

Refreshment from the water of life,

Inner calm from the peace of God;

All you do be within the love of God,

Nowhere you go be without God's blessing.

Bridget (f) comes from the Irish Gaelic meaning 'exalted one' or 'shining bright'.

Brightly may God shine upon you,

Richly may he bless you,

Intimately may he understand you,

Deeply may he love you,

Gently may he lead you,

Eternally may he keep you,

Tenderly may he embrace you.

Bronwen (f) comes from two Welsh words meaning 'breast' and 'white' or in combination, 'fair-breasted'. For Bronwyn (f) see appendix.

Before you the blessing of God to guide you,

Round you the blessing of God to embrace you,

Over you the blessing of God to shelter you,

Near you the blessing of God to protect you,

Within you the blessing of God to strengthen you,

Every blessing of God to keep you,

Now and always, in his love.

Brooke (f), and Brooklyn (m/f) come from the word for a small stream of water. The first two lines refer to John 4.14 & 10. For Brook (m) omit the last line.

Blessings from the wellspring of life be with you,

Refreshment from the living waters be within you,

On you be the peace of the lake's still waters,

On you be the sparkle of the brook's running waters,

Kind blessings from the source of love to you,

Eternal blessings from the God of life to you.

Blessings from the wellspring of life be with you,

Refreshment from the living waters be within you,

On you be the peace of the lake's still waters,

On you be the sparkle of the brook's running waters,

Kind blessings from the source of love to you;

Let the healing waters of God's love wash over

Your body, mind and soul, bringing you

New blessings each new day.

Bryony (f) comes from the wild hedgerow plant of the same name. For Briony (f) see appendix.

Bless Bryony,

Risen Lord Jesus;

Your blessing of peace be on her,

On her be your blessing of joy,

Newness of life be within her;

Your love be with her forever.

Caitlin (f) is an Irish form of Katherine which may derive from the Greek *katharos* meaning 'pure'. The fifth and sixth lines refer to Zechariah 13.9. A variant spelling is Kaitlin (f). For Katelyn (f) see appendix.

Christ Jesus bless you

And keep you pure in heart

In every trial and temptation.

The Lord God grant you perfect peace,

Like silver refined of all impurity

In the fire of his love,

Now and always.

CALLUM – *meaning Dove, a symbol of the Holy Spirit.*

Caleb (m) is a Hebrew name meaning 'intrepid and bold', or possibly meaning a 'dog' (suggesting devotion). In the Bible, Caleb was a leader alongside Joshua as the Israelites entered the promised land (Numbers 14.24 & Deuteronomy 1.36).

Courage to stand up for what is right,

And boldness to explore what is new,

Love of God, of neighbour and of self:

Eternal God bestow all these gifts upon Caleb,

Bless him and bring him to the promised land.

Callum (m) is derived from Columba, meaning 'dove' – a symbol of the Holy Spirit (Mark 1.10). The third and fourth lines refer to the day of Pentecost (Acts 2.1–4).

Come upon Callum, Spirit of God,

As the dove to bring him your peace,

Like the fire to inflame him with your love,

Like the rushing wind to fill him with your inspiration;

Untamed wind, unquenchable fire, unconquerable peace,

May your blessings be with Callum always.

Cameron (m/f) is a Scottish clan name (meaning 'crooked nose').
The second line of this prayer refers to John 10.10.

Constant the love of God to you,

Abundant the life from God to you,

Manifold the gifts of God to you,

Everlasting the light of God upon you,

Rich the blessings of God for you,

Overflowing the joy of God to you,

Never-ending the peace of God within you.

Camilla (f) comes from the Latin meaning 'attendant at a
sacrifice'.

Christ be beside you,

Above you, beneath you;

May his peace abide

In the depths of your being;

Let his light shine before you,

Let his love shine within you,

And his blessings be ever upon you.

Cara (f) means 'dear' or 'dear one' (from the Latin or Irish).

Caring God, be with Cara

Awake and asleep, all the hours of the day,

Resting and working, all the days of the year,

As a child and adult, all the years of her life.

Carla (f) is a feminine version of Karl (itself a German form of Charles). For Carly (f) see appendix.

Constantly may God guard you,

Ardently may God love you,

Richly may God bless you,

Loyally may God remain to you

A friend and saviour forever.

Carole (f) and Caroline (f) derive from Charles. However these prayers play upon the verbal link with 'carol' which originally meant a circling or ring dance. For Carol (f) and Carolyn (f) see appendix.

Circle Carole with your blessings, Lord,

And dance with her in your joy;

Ring her round with your protection,

O Lord, surround her with your peace.

Let your love embrace her for ever;

Encircle her, Lord, with your blessings.

Circle Caroline with your blessings, Lord,

And dance with her in your joy;

Ring her round with your protection,

O Lord, surround her with your care.

Let her steps always remain

In the circumference of your peace;

Now and forever embrace her, Lord,

Encircle her with your love.

Catherine (f) may derive from the Greek *katharos* meaning 'pure'. According to legend St. Catherine of Alexandria (4th century) was tortured upon a wheel, hence the firework called a Catherine wheel. This prayer makes reference to John 10.10 & Deuteronomy 33.27.

Creator God bless you

And grant you fullness of life;

The King of Love bless you,

Hold you in his everlasting arms;

Eternal Father bless you,

Remain with you always;

Inextinguishable Light bless you,

Now and always guide you,

Evermore shine upon you.

Celia (f) derives from the Latin *caelum* meaning 'heaven'.

Crucified Jesus, bear your pain,

Easter Christ, renew your life,

Light of the world, shine upon you,

Immortal love, bless you and keep you,

Ascended Lord, raise you heavenwards.

Charles (m) means 'free man' (from the German Karl). Charlotte (f) and its shortened form of Lottie (f) derive from Charles. For Charlie (m/f) see appendix.

Christ Jesus, bless Charles:

Help him when he feels

Anxious or afraid;

Reassure him when he is

Lost or lacking in confidence;

Encourage and equip him in each

Successive stage of life.

Caring God, walk with Charlotte,

Heal her when she is hurt,

Accompany her when she is lonely,

Rescue her when she is in trouble,

Lead her when she is lost,

Overcome every obstacle,

Teach her your way,

Travelling with her

Every step of life's journey.

Lord, by your blessing keep Lottie

Open hearted and open minded,

True to herself,

Thoughtful of others,

Interested in the wonders of your world,

Every day of her life.

Chelsea (f) comes from a London place name meaning 'landing place for limestone'.

Centre of all things, dwell within Chelsea,

Heart of life, pulse through her being,

Essence of love, flavour her nature,

Light of light, shine brightly upon her,

Source of all goodness, well up in her soul,

Everlasting peace, keep her in your care,

Almighty God, bless her forever.

The name Cheryl (f) was formed from a combination of Cherry and Beryl.

Cherishing God,

Hold Cheryl in your love,

Encourage her when she falters,

Raise her up when she falls,

Yoke her spirit to yours,

Lavish your blessings upon her.

Chloe (f) comes from the Greek, meaning 'young shoot'. Chloe and her household were early converts of St. Paul (1 Corinthians 1.11).

Caring God, hold Chloe in your arms,

Holding God, encircle her with love,

Loving God, watch over her,

Over-watching God, encourage her,

Encouraging God, keep her in your care.

Christine (f), Christina (f) and Christian (m) all come from the Latin 'Christianus' meaning a Christian (Christ is the Greek translation of the Hebrew *Messiah*, both words meaning 'anointed one'). According to the Bible it was in Antioch that 'the disciples were for the first time called Christians' (Acts 11.26, RSV). The word appears to have been coined by Romans and used scornfully but followers of Christ soon adopted the word with pride (see 1 Peter 4.16). For Christina (f) see appendix.

Christ Jesus be in your heart, as

He holds you forever in his,

Raising you up, when you are brought low,

In the power of his resurrection.

So may the Bread of Life feed you,

The Light of the World lead you

In the way, the truth and the life,

Now and here,

Everywhere and always.

Christ Jesus be in your heart, as

He holds you forever in his,

Raising you up, when you are brought low,

In the power of his resurrection.

So may the bread of life feed you,

The light of the world lead you

In the way, the truth and the life,

And the good shepherd bless you,

Now and always. Amen.

Christopher (m) means 'Christ-carrier' (from the Greek).
According to legend, St. Christopher carried the young Jesus across
a river. As a result St. Christopher has become the patron saint of
travellers.

Carry Christopher in your loving arms, as

He carries your name, Christ Jesus, in his.

Raise him up when he falters or falls

In distress or disappointment.

Shield and sustain him

Through dearth and danger.

On all his journey through life

Prosper his way and grant him

Health, hope and happiness,

Even until his path

Reaches his home with you in heaven.

Clare (f) comes from the Latin *clarus* meaning 'pure' or 'clear'. For Claire and Clara (f) see appendix.

Clear as the cloudless sky, God's peace to you,

Like the breeze off the ocean, God's life for you,

As bright as a mountain stream, God's joy to you,

Refreshing as pure spring water, God's spirit within you,

Even more than the myriad stars, God's blessings to you.

Colette (f) is a diminutive of the French name Nicolette. Cole (m) also may come from Nicholas, or from the Old English meaning 'swarthy'. For Cole see appendix.

Christ guard and guide you

On every path which lies before you;

Let the light of Christ illuminate

Every step you take;

The love of God be within you,

The blessing of God be upon you

Every day of your life.

Colin (m) is a shortened form of Nicholas.

Christ's blessing be upon you,

On all your words and works;

Let the peace of Christ be within you,

In your thoughts and dreams;

Now and here, everywhere and always.

Connor (m) is an Irish name meaning 'hunter' (literally 'lover of hounds or wolves').

Creator God and caring Father,

Origin of life and love,

Nurture in Connor a loving, caring nature,

Never leave him to face temptations alone,

Open for him the way to fulfilment and peace,

Remain with him every day of his life.

Cooper (m) comes from the occupational name 'barrel maker'. This prayer makes reference to the wedding at Cana (John 2.1–11), the feeding of the five thousand (John 6.1–14) and 2 Corinthians 4.7.

Christ Jesus' life-changing blessings be

On you and within you:

Out of your water may he make wine;

Provide a feast from your loaves and fishes;

Entrust his treasure to your earthen vessel;

Raise you with him to newness of life.

Corey (m) may either mean 'God's peace', or a 'hill' or 'hollow'.

Christ before you, Christ behind you,

Over you, beneath you,

Round you, within you;

Every day and evermore

Your guide and guard, your love and Lord.

Courtney (f) comes from the French place name, Courtenay.
This prayer makes reference to Psalm 84.10.

Creator God, in whose courts

One day is better than a thousand,

Under whose care we find

Refreshment for our souls,

Touch Courtney with your love,

Nurture her with your peace,

Enrich her with your joy and send

Your blessings on her evermore.

Craig (m) comes from the Scottish Gaelic for 'crag'.

Crucified Jesus, bear your pain,

Risen Jesus, raise you up,

Ascended Jesus, look on you with love,

Immortal Jesus, be with you forever,

Gracious Jesus, grant you peace.

Crispin (m) comes from the Latin *crispus* meaning 'curly haired'. 'Refugee Christ' refers to the time Jesus and his parents spent in Egypt, having fled there for safety from Herod (Matthew 2.13–15).

Christ of the manger, be born in you,

Refugee Christ, guard you and guide you,

Incarnate Christ, walk beside you,

Suffering Christ, share your pain,

Persecuted Christ, give you his courage,

Immortal Christ, raise you to new life,

Never-ending Christ, bless you always.

———————

The name, Daisy (f), comes from the flower and means 'day's eye'.

Dear God, shine upon Daisy each day:

As the eye of the flower opens

In the light and warmth of the sun,

So may your love open the eyelids of her heart,

Your blessings unfurl the petals of her soul.

Daniel (m) and Danielle (f) come from the Hebrew meaning 'God is judge'. The Old Testament book of Daniel contains both the prophecies by him and the stories about him, including his being thrown into a pit with lions because he refused to stop worshipping God (Daniel 6). For Daniella (f) see appendix.

Dear God, be with Daniel,

Above him to watch over him,

Near him to protect him,

In him to inspire and instruct him,

Embracing him with your love,

Leading him on his life-long journey.

Dear God, be with Danielle,

Above her to watch over her,

Near her to protect her,

In her to inspire and instruct her,

Embracing her with your love,

Leading her on her life-long journey.

Let your blessing be upon her

Evermore and evermore.

The name Darren (m) is of uncertain origin, possibly from Darryl.

Deep peace of God encircle you

And deep hope of God encourage you

Rich gifts of God enable you

Rich blessings of God endow you

Everlasting light of God enhance you

Never-ending love of God enfold you.

David (m) comes from the Hebrew meaning 'beloved'. The story of David, from the shepherd boy who killed Goliath to the greatest king of Israel, is told in the first and second books of Samuel (starting at 1 Samuel 16).

Deeper than the deepest mystery,

As close as your deepest desire,

Vaster than the deepest reaches of space,

Infinite yet intimate may God's love for you be,

Daily yet eternal the blessings of God upon you.

Deborah (f) comes from the Hebrew for 'bee', and so means 'diligent and hardworking'. Deborah was a prophet and one of the judges of Israel (Judges 4.4). For Debra (f) see appendix.

Day by day, God grow within you,

Evening by evening, God refresh you,

Blessing after blessing God lavish upon you,

On and on, God's love endure for you,

Round and round, God's protection encircle you,

Arm in arm, God walk with you,

Heart to heart, God be close to you.

Diligent be God's care for you,

Enduring be God's love for you,

Bright be God's light upon you,

Beautiful be God's gifts to you,

Invincible be God's protection around you,

Eternal be God's life within you.

Dennis (m) and Denise (f) derive from the Greek, Dionysios, meaning a follower of Dionysos the Greek God of wine. Dionysios or 'Denis the Areopagite' is mentioned as a follower of Saint Paul in Acts 17.34. This prayer refers to Jesus' miracle at the wedding at Cana (John 2.1–11). For Denis (m) omit the fourth line of Dennis.

Dear Jesus, bless Dennis:

Even as you turned water into wine,

Now enrich and transform his nature,

Nurturing in him your newness of life,

Investing within him your

Spirit of love and joy and peace.

Dear Jesus,

Even as you turned water into wine,

Now transform Denise's nature,

Investing within her your

Spirit of love and joy and peace,

Enriching her with your blessings.

Derek (m) is an English and shortened form of the German Theodoric (which means 'ruler of the people').

Daily may God bless you,

Eternally keep you in his peace,

Repeatedly may God forgive you,

Eternally keep you in his mercy,

Keep you eternally in his love.

The name Destiny (f) comes from the word meaning 'fate' or 'end and purpose'. This prayer derives from an old Celtic blessing of peace.

Deep peace of the running wave to you,

Eternal peace of the shining stars to you,

Strong peace of the quiet earth to you,

True peace of the flowing air to you,

Infinite peace of the Spirit of peace to you,

Never-ending peace of the Son of peace to you,

Your blessing of peace from the God of peace to you.

Diana (f) was the Roman goddess of the moon and the hunt. The prayers for Diana and Diane (f) explore different Biblical imagery for the Holy Spirit. For Diane omit 'And' in the last line.

Descend, Holy Spirit, and bless Diana,

Inspire her with your breath of life,

Alight on her with your wings of peace,

Nourish her with the Word of God,

And enflame her with your tongues of fire.

Dominic (m) comes originally from the Latin, *dominus*, meaning 'lord'. The earliest Christian creed is simply 'Jesus is Lord' (Romans 10.9 & Philippians 2.11). St. Dominic (1170–1221) founded the Dominican Order (also known as Black Friars). Domincans were, and still are, characterised by devotion to study and preaching.

Dearest Lord, look with favour

On your faithful servant, Dominic;

Master and saviour, pour your love

Into his heart and soul and mind;

Now send him out to live and work

In the power of your Spirit, to your praise and glory;

Christ Jesus, bless him and keep him always.

Donald (m) comes from the Scottish Gaelic meaning 'world mighty', 'great chief' or 'proud ruler'.

Deep within you, the peace of God,

Over you, the blessing of God,

Near you, the protection of God,

Around you, the embrace of God,

Leading you forward, the guidance of God,

Drawing you nearer, the love of God.

Deep within you, the peace of God;

Over you his blessing; beneath you his support;

Near you his defence; before you his guidance.

Dorothy (f) comes from the Greek and means 'gift of God'.

Dove-like Spirit, descend upon you,

Offering you gifts of courage and peace;

Risen Jesus, raise you up,

Offering you gifts of life and joy;

The God of love abide within you,

Hope and faith his gifts to you,

Yet greater than these, his love.

Douglas (m) means 'black water or stream' and is Scottish in origin.

Deepen your peace within Douglas, Lord,

Over him watch and guide,

Under him give your strong support,

Good Lord, embrace him with your love,

Let your blessings be with him

And may your light

Shine upon him for ever.

Dudley (m) comes from an English place name meaning 'people's field'.

Day by day, send your blessings

Upon Dudley, Lord God;

Decade by decade,

Let your love grow within his heart;

Evermore and evermore, grant him

Your mercy, your peace and your joy.

Duncan (m) comes from the Gaelic meaning 'dark warrior' or 'dark-skinned chief'.

Deep peace of God to you

Unfading light of God to you

Never-ending hope of God to you

Constant love of God to you

Abundant life of God to you

Numberless blessings of God to you.

Dylan (m) is a Welsh name derived from the Celtic words for 'flood' and 'sea'.

Dear Father,

You give us to each other.

Let Dylan's parents be to him his walls and roof,

And he to them a door to new joy,

Now and forever, Amen.

Edward (m) is derived from the Old English *ead* meaning 'rich'
or 'blessed', and *weard* which means to 'guard'.

Encircle Edward with your love,

Defend him from all deceit or danger

Which may hurt his body or harm his soul;

And direct him in the ways of justice,

Righteousness and peace,

Dearest God, our guardian and guide.

Eileen (f) is the Irish form of Helen.

Everlasting be God's light upon you

Infinite his grace

Long and deep God's peace within you

Eternal be his hope

Endless be God's love for you

Never-ending his blessings.

Elaine (f) comes from the Old French form of Helen.

Everlasting be God's light upon you

Long and deep his peace

Always be God's hope within you

Infinite his grace

Never-ending be God's love for you

Endless his blessings.

Eleanor (f) derives from a French form of Helen. This prayer evokes the great sequence of Christian festivals, telling the story from Christ's birth to his sending of the Holy Spirit. The last line is a reference to Jesus' parting words in Matthew's gospel (Matthew 28.20).

Epiphany God, reveal yourself to Eleanor,

Lenten Lord, be with her in temptation,

Easter God, raise her to fullness of life,

Ascended Lord, reign in her heart.

Now, as at Pentecost, send your Spirit

On Eleanor, and may your blessing

Remain with her always, to the end of time.

Elijah (m) is a Hebrew name meaning 'Yahweh is God'. Elijah is one of the most important prophets in the Old Testament, living during the 9th century BC. His story begins at 1 Kings 17.1 and ends with his being taken up to heaven in a whirlwind (2 Kings 2.11). In the New Testament Elijah appears, along with Moses, beside Jesus in his transfiguration (Mark 9.4) and John the Baptist is associated with Elijah (Mark 9.11–13; John 1.21) because of a belief that Elijah would come again as a forerunner to the Messiah. This prayer echoes the prayer known as 'the Grace' (2 Corinthians 13.14).

Every day and everywhere,

Let the love of God be with you;

In all you do and think and say,

Jesus' grace be with you;

And may the fellowship of God's

Holy Spirit be with you evermore.

Elizabeth (f) comes from the Hebrew name meaning 'God has sworn' or 'consecrated to God'. In the Bible Elizabeth is the mother of John the Baptist and kinswoman of Mary, mother of Jesus (Luke 1). Betty (f) is a shortened form of Elizabeth. For Eliza (f) see appendix.

Embrace Elizabeth in your grace,

Loving and life-giving Lord.

Inspire and increase in her

Zest for life and zeal for

All good things.

Bless her and keep her,

Encircle her with love,

That she may enjoy

Health and happiness always.

Better than riches, God grant you wisdom,

Excelling all wishes, God give you his blessing,

Truer than any guide, God show you the way,

Tenderer than the gentlest touch, God comfort you,

Yet best of all, God give you his love.

Ella (f) comes from the German meaning 'all'.

Every blessing of God be upon you:

Let the peace of God be in all your thinking;

Let the love of God be in all your meeting;

And the joy of God be in all your fulfilling.

Ellie (f) is a diminutive of Helen, Eleanor or Ella.

East, west, north and south,

Learning, loving, working and resting,

Let your blessing be on Ellie, Lord,

In everything she does,

Everywhere she goes.

Elliot (m) comes from Elijah (via the Greek form, Elias). For
Eliott (m) and Elliott (m) see appendix.

Every moment of each day,

Let the peace of God give you strength,

Let the strength of God protect you,

In your heart may the love of God abide,

Over your ways may the God of love preside,

The blessings of God be ever upon you.

Ellis (m/f) may derive from Elias (the Greek form of Elijah), or from the Irish Eilis, or the Welsh *elus* meaning 'kind'.

Every morning, in your rising,

Let your heart be full of God's loving kindness;

Let your soul be full of God's gentle peace,

In your resting, every evening:

So may God bless you, every day of your life.

————————

Emilia (f) is the Italian form of Emily.

Every day of your life,

May God bless you,

Encourage and equip you,

Lead and enlighten you,

Instruct and inspire you,

And accompany you always.

————————

Emily (f) comes from the Latin for 'eager'.

Embrace Emily in your love and protection,

Maker, mender and miracle-worker God;

In all her learning, loving, living and giving

Let her be eager to know and do

Your will and your work.

Emma (f) is derived from the old German meaning 'entire' and 'universal'. Emmanuel is one of the Hebrew titles given to Jesus and means 'God with us' (Matthew 1.23).

Even he who made the entire universe,

Maker of all life and everything that is,

May he make known his love for you,

And abide with you, your Lord Emmanuel.

Eoghan (m) is an Irish and Scottish name, possibly meaning 'yew' or 'born', or possibly an Irish form of Eugene or Owen.

Even before you were born, God loved you,

Or you were conceived, God knew you.

God bring to birth in you

His peace, his joy, his goodness,

And bless you even before you ask

Now and always.

Eric (m) comes from the Norse (Erik) combining two words, the first meaning either 'forever' or 'one' or 'alone', and the second meaning 'ruler'.

Evermore may God guard you,

Rule in your heart with love.

In God alone may you find true peace;

Christ bless you and keep you forever.

Erin (f) is an Irish name, related to Eire – the name for Ireland itself.

Every morning, in your waking,

Rise with the risen Christ within you;

In your resting, every evening,

Nightly blessings of God be upon you.

Ernest (m) means 'earnest', 'determined' or 'serious' (from the German).

Endless be God's blessings upon you,

Rich his gifts of grace to you,

Never-sleeping his watch of care over you,

Evermore his love for you,

Swift and sure his help for you,

Trustworthy and true his promises to you.

———————

Esme (f) comes from the Old French and means 'esteemed' or 'beloved'.

Even as God esteems you highly,

So may you see the best in others:

May you bless and love your neighbour,

Even as God loves and blesses you greatly.

Ethan (m) is from the Hebrew for 'constant', 'firm', 'strong' or 'long-lived'. Ethan the Ezrahite is mentioned in the Bible (1 Kings 4.31) for his wisdom, and is credited as the author of Psalm 89.

Eternal God, bless Ethan,

True God, may he hold firm to what is right,

Holy God, give him strength of faith,

Almighty God, let him be constant in his loving,

Nurturing God, grant him health and long life.

Evan (m) is a Welsh name, either a Welsh equivalent of John, or from the Celtic meaning 'young warrior'.

Everlasting the light of God for you,

Vast and deep the love of God for you,

Abundant the blessings of God for you,

Never-ending the life of God for you.

EVE – *everywhere she sails on the sea of life.*

Eve (f), the first woman in the Bible and companion to Adam, comes from the Hebrew meaning 'living' (Genesis 3.20) because she is the mother of all living beings. For Evie (f) and Eva (f) see appendix.

Everywhere she sails on the sea of life, guide Eve's

Vessel safely through fog and storm and strait,

Even until she reaches her haven with you.

———————

The name Evelyn (m/f) may be used for either sex. As a girl's name it may come from a combination of 'Eve' and 'Lynn'.

Everlasting be God's love for you,

Very many and great his gifts to you,

Endless be his blessings upon you.

Let the peace of God fill

Your heart and mind and soul,

Now and for evermore.

———————

Ewan (m) is the English version of the Gaelic Eoghan – also connected to Owen.

Everything good comes from you, Lord God:

We thank you for the gift of Ewan's life,

Asking that you may bless him with health and happiness,

Now and always. Amen.

Faith (f) is named after the virtue. To have faith in God means both to believe in his presence and to trust in his love. According to St. Paul, faith is one of the three great abiding virtues: faith, hope and love (1 Corinthians 13.13). This prayer is based on the prayer by Satish Kumar known as 'the Peace Prayer'.

From death to life may God lead you,

And from falsehood to truth,

Into hope from despair, from fear to faith,

To love from hate, and from war to peace:

Holy God, lead you and bless you.

Felicity (f) comes from the Latin meaning 'happiness' or 'good fortune'.

Fulfilled be your life,

Eternal God's life within you;

Lasting be your loves,

Infinite God's love for you;

Clear be your light,

Inextinguishable God's light upon you;

The blessings of God be ever upon you,

Your happiness be evermore in him.

Findlay (m) comes from the Gaelic meaning 'fair warrior'.
For Finlay (m) and Finley (m) see appendix.

First may God bless you

In your years of growing and learning to live,

Next may God bless you

During the years of working and learning to give,

Lastly may God bless you

As you approach the final days of your life,

Your years well spent and richly blessed.

Finn (m) means 'white' or 'fair' (from the Irish Gaelic).

Fair be the prospect before you,

Invincible God's protection around you,

Noble the hopes within you,

Numberless God's blessings upon you.

Fiona (f) means 'white' or 'fair' (from the Gaelic).

From falsehood may God lead you to truth,

In darkness may God bring you to light,

On your journey may God show you his way,

Nearer may God draw you into his love,

All your days may God bless you and keep you.

Florence (f) comes from the Latin *florens* meaning 'blossoming', 'flowering' or 'flourishing'.

Father God bless you,

Let the warmth of his love, like sunshine,

Open the buds and blossom of your nature,

Ripen the fruit of your spirit,

Establish and deepen your roots.

Now and always may you flourish,

Constantly may God nourish you,

Evermore cherish you.

The names Francis (m), Frances (f) and Francesca (f) have the root meaning 'French'. It is said that St. Francis of Assisi (1181–1226) was baptised as John but was called Francis because he was born while his father was in France. From a wealthy family, Francis gave up his inheritance and lived a life of simplicity, founding the Franciscan Order of Friars. These prayers are based on the famous prayer attributed to St. Francis. For Frances see appendix.

Father, bless Francis and let him bring

Reconciliation where there is discord,

Affection where there is coldness of heart,

New hope where there is despair,

Comfort where there is sadness,

Illumination where there is darkness,

So may he be an instrument of your peace.

Father, bless Francesca and let her bring

Reconciliation where there is discord,

Affection where there is coldness of heart,

New hope where there is despair,

Comfort where there is sadness.

Eternal Master, grant that she may never seek

So much to be loved as to love,

Consoled as to console,

And so make her an instrument of your peace.

Frank (m) developed as a shortened form of Francis (or Franklin) but is now considered a name in its own right.

From all that is false may God lead you to truth,

Release you from all that restrains your spirit,

Against all that is evil may God defend you.

Now and always may God bless you,

Keeping you forever in his love and his peace.

Freddie (m), now a popular name in its own right, is a shortened version either of Frederick or Alfred.

From everything false, deliver Freddie,

Rescue him from all that is wrong,

Expel from his path all that is evil,

Defend him from every danger.

Direct him towards truth and life,

In the way that leads to you,

Eternal God, for evermore.

Frederick (m) is derived from Old German and means 'peaceful ruler'.

From everything false, deliver Frederick,

Rescue him from all that is wrong,

Expel from his path all that is evil,

Direct him in the way of truth and life;

Every day lead him and guide him,

Reach out to him in every need,

In every danger defend him,

Christ Jesus, bless him evermore,

Keep him in your peace and your love.

Freya (f) was the Norse goddess of love, after whom Friday is named.

Father of all, and fount of all goodness,

Remain with Freya and bless her

Every day of her life, for with

You we can lack nothing.

Amen.

Gabriel (m) means 'my strength is in God' in Hebrew and is the name of the angel who appeared to Zechariah (Luke 1.8–20) and to Mary (Luke 1.26–38) to bring them the news that they would each soon have a son. Gabriel also appears in the book of Daniel (Dan. 8.16–26 and 9.20–27). The prayers for Gabriel, Gabriella (f) and Gabrielle (f) echo the words of the song of the angel who appeared to the shepherds (Luke 2.14) to tell them of Jesus' birth (although, in fact, the Bible does not give this angel a name). For Gabrielle see appendix.

Glory to God in the highest,

And peace on earth to you whom he loves.

Blessings of God be in your spirit,

Righteousness of God in your heart,

In your understanding be God's wisdom,

Everything you do be in God's strength;

Let his glory shine upon you always.

Glory to God in the highest,

And peace on earth to you whom he loves.

Blessings of God be in your spirit,

Righteousness of God in your heart,

In your understanding be God's wisdom,

Everything you do be in God's strength,

Let the grace of God be ever with you,

Let the love of God be ever within you,

And may God's glory shine ever upon you.

Gail (f) is a shortened form of Abigail (which means 'Father's joy').

God give you blessings of joy in your sadness,

And blessings of plenty in your need;

In your family and friendships, blessings of love;

Let your whole life be blessed with God's peace.

The name Gareth (m) comes from the Welsh meaning 'gentle'.

Gentleness to you from the God of love,

And strength to you from the God of power;

Rest to you from the dove-like Spirit,

Energy to you from the wind of the Spirit;

True life to you from the risen Son,

Happiness from the source of every true joy.

Gary (m) derives from the Germanic *gar* meaning 'spear'. This prayer links the idea of a weapon to St. Paul's description of the whole armour of God (Ephesians 6.11–17).

God grant you his armour to guard against evil,

And give you his belt of truth, his shoes of peace;

Righteousness be your breastplate, faith your shield,

Your helmet God's salvation, his Spirit your sword.

Gavin (m) is an Anglicised version of the Welsh name Gawain which may in turn derive from the Welsh for 'hawk'.

God give you wings of faith to rise

Above the snares of temptation and sin,

Vanity and selfishness,

Into the clear blue sky of God's

Never-ending love.

Gemma (f) means 'gem' or 'jewel' (from the Italian).

Great the blessings of God for you,

Eternal the life of God within you,

Much the joy, little the sadness,

Many the friends, few the troubles,

And steadfast the love of God for you.

Geoffrey (m) comes from the old German meaning 'peace' or 'peaceful ruler'. For Geoff omit the last three lines.

God's blessings be

Ever upon you;

Over you may he ever watch;

Forever may his peace flow upon you,

Forever may his love grow within you;

Rising every day, may God renew your hope,

Every night may he be

Your source of rest and refreshment.

George (m) comes from the Greek *georgos* meaning 'farmer'. George is the patron saint of England. For Georgia (f) and Georgina (f) see appendix.

> **G**od of life, sow your blessings in the
>
> **E**arth of George's spirit,
>
> **O**ver time may they send down
>
> **R**oots deep and sustaining,
>
> **G**rowing an abundant harvest of all things
>
> **E**xcellent, true, pure and gracious.

Gerald (m) derives from the Germanic *gar* meaning 'spear'. The prayer for Gerald links the idea of a weapon to St. Paul's description of the whole armour of God (Ephesians 6.11–17). For Geraldine (f) see appendix.

> **G**od grant you his armour to guard against evil,
>
> **E**quip you with the belt of truth and shoes of peace;
>
> **R**ighteousness be your breastplate
>
> **A**nd your helmet be God's salvation;
>
> **L**et one hand hold the shield of faith,
>
> **D**rawing with the other the sword of the Spirit.

Gerry (m) is a shortened form of Gerald and Gerard.

God bless you,

Enfold you in his love,

Reach out to you when you are in need,

Raise you when you fall;

Your life be filled with his peace.

Gillian (f) probably comes from Julian. For Gill (f) see appendix.

God bless you and dwell within you,

In your heart may his love make a home,

Let his peace abide in each room of your life,

Let his joy find a place at your table,

In your spirit may his Spirit ever remain,

And from the windows of your soul

Now and always may his light shine forth.

Glynn (m) and Glyn (m) come from the Welsh for 'valley'. For Glyn omit the fourth line.

God, the giver of all good things,

Let your love dwell within Glynn's heart,

Your peace abide within his soul,

Nowhere may he go without your protection,

Never may he be without your blessing.

Gordon (m) comes from a Celtic place name meaning 'large fort'. This prayer refers to Psalm 18.2 (RSV): 'The Lord is my rock, and my fortress'.

God be your strong fortress:

On every side your walls of defence,

Rock beneath you, and your shelter above.

Day by day may God bless and love you,

Over all your ways may God watch and guide you,

Now and forever may God keep you in peace.

Grace (f) comes from the Latin *gratia* meaning 'favour'. In the Bible it means more specifically the free gift of God's favour and mercy towards us, given not because of our merits but out of his generous love for us. 'The grace' may mean a prayer of thanks before a meal, or may refer to the Trinitarian prayer from 2 Corinthians 13.14. For Gracie (f) see appendix.

God grant you his generous gifts of grace,

Riches beyond price, yet freely given;

Abundant life, unconditional love,

Countless blessings, perfect peace,

Enduring hope and joy without end.

Graham (m) comes from a place name (meaning 'Granta's homestead' or 'gravelly homestead'). This prayer is based on the words of the Millennium resolution – the last words to be heard on BBC Radio 4 before the year 2000 began.

God give you love in your life,

Respect for the earth

And peace towards all people,

Healing of past wrongs

And delight in the good;

May God bless you anew each day.

Gwendoline (f) comes from two Welsh words, the first meaning 'fair', 'white' or 'blessed' and the second meaning 'ring' or 'bow'. In combination they may suggest the moon. The opening of this prayer refers to Paul's letter to the Romans 12.15. For Gwen (f) see appendix.

God weep with you when you are weeping,

When you rejoice, rejoice with you;

Enrich you when you are poor in spirit,

Nourish you when your soul is in want,

Defend you when you are in danger,

Open to you when you seek and knock,

Lead you when you lose your way,

Illuminate you when darkness surrounds you,

Night after night may God bless your resting,

Each morning may you rise to newness of life.

Gwyneth and Gwynneth (f) come from the Welsh meaning
'happiness' or 'good fortune'. For Gwyneth omit the fourth line.

God weep with you when you are weeping,

When you rejoice, rejoice with you;

Your burdens ease when you are weary,

Nourish and nurture you when you are weak;

Night after night may God bless your resting,

Each new day may he bless your rising;

The blessing of God grant you

Health and happiness always.

Hamish (m) is a Scottish Gaelic form of James.

Holy God be with Hamish always,

Always defend him with your might,

Mighty God grant him inspiration,

Inspire him with your Holy Spirit,

Spirit of God increase his holiness,

Holy God bless Hamish always.

HARLEY – *from the place name meaning hare meadow.*

Hannah (f) is a Hebrew name meaning 'grace' or 'favour'. In the Bible, Hannah is the mother of Samuel (1 Book of Samuel 1–2) whom she recognises as a gracious gift from God and an answer to her prayer when she was barren.

Heavenly Father, bless Hannah

And accompany her on the path of life;

Neither let her foot stumble

Nor let her lose sight of the way;

And at the end of her journey welcome her home,

Her hopes fulfilled and her heart content.

Harley (m) comes from a place name meaning 'hare meadow'.

Highly may God favour you

And deeply may he love you;

Rightly may he guide you,

Lightly may he correct you;

Eternally may he keep you

Yet daily may he bless you.

Harriet (f), Harry (m) and Harrison (m) are all derived from Henry, meaning 'owner of a home'.

Holy God bless you and raise you,

Above all that is shallow or selfish raise you,

Raise you from falsehood to truth,

Raise you from despair to hope,

In sadness raise you to joy,

Even from death raise you

To the risen life of his Son.

Heavenly Father,

As you raised your son from death to life,

Raise Harrison from falsehood to truth,

Raise him from despair to hope,

In times of fear raise him to trust.

Should he stumble, raise him in your love,

Out of darkness raise him to your light,

Now and always keep him in your peace.

Heavenly Father,

As you raised your son from death,

Raise Harry from every fall,

Renew in him each day and year

Your Easter life and peace and joy.

Harvey (m) means 'battle worthy' (from the Breton Gaelic). This prayer refers to the spiritual defences which Paul describes as the 'whole armour of God' (Ephesians 6.11 & 13, RSV).

Heavenly Father, bless Harvey and grant him

Armour fitting for the challenges he will face:

Righteousness to fight against injustice,

Virtue to defend him against evil,

Endurance to sustain him when the battle is long,

Your love, above all, which can never be defeated.

Hayden (m) means 'hedged valley'.

Here and everywhere, God bless you,

Always and now, God be with you,

Young and old, God support you,

Day and night, God love you,

East and west, God guide you,

North and south, God keep you safe.

Hayley (f) comes from the old English place name meaning a 'hay meadow'. For Haley (f) and Hailey (f) see appendix.

Holy God, hold Hayley in your love

And enfold her in your peace,

Your comfort, your protection.

Let your blessing be on her daily;

Every night your blessing of rest,

Your blessing of new life every rising.

Heather (f) is named after the moorland flower.

He who covers the hills in heather,

Embrace and clothe you in his love;

As the moors turn purple with heather's bloom,

The God of love nurture your soul into flower;

He whose spring brings new life and light,

Even so may he renew you and bless you

Richly, abundantly and deeply.

Heidi (f) is a shortened form of the German Adelheid (from which we derive Adelaide), meaning 'of noble birth'.

Hide yourself deep within Heidi, Lord,

Establish your roots in her soul,

Invest your love and hope in her heart,

Dwell with your peace in her spirit,

Inhabit her whole being with blessings.

Helen (f) comes from the Greek for sun (*helios*) and so has the meaning of bright or shining light. St. Helena (c.250–330) was the mother of Constantine, the first Christian emperor of Rome. According to mediaeval beliefs she came originally from England. The last line refers to Philippians 2.9. For Helena (f) and Helene (f) see appendix.

Heavenly Father, bless Helen now and to eternity,

Eternal God, guide her with your light,

Light of the world, shine on her with Easter glory,

Easter Lord, give her new life in your name,

Name above all names, bring her safely to heaven.

Henry (m) means 'home owner' (from the German Heinrich). For Henrietta (f) see appendix.

Home to our restless hearts, God draw you to his love;

Ear to our spirit's voice, God listen to your longings;

Nourishment to our deepest hungers, God feed you and feast you,

Refreshment to our weary souls, God give you fullness of life,

Yes to our yearnings, God answer you with blessings.

Hermione (f) is a Greek name, the feminine version of Hermes, the Greek messenger of the gods. The Bible makes many references to God's hands as a symbol of his action upon earth: e.g. Psalms 63.8, 98.1, 139.10.

Hold Hermione in your hands, Lord,

Embrace her in your love,

Reach out to her in her need.

May your hands, which made her,

Inwardly heal her,

Outwardly protect her,

Never let go of her,

Evermore bless her.

Hilary (f/m) derives from the Latin *hilaris* meaning 'cheerful'. For the male version please change the pronouns.

Holy God, bless Hilary;

In her sadness let there be hope,

Let there be cheerfulness even in troubles,

And let there be light in her darkness,

Rainbows through her rain,

Your love and life even beyond death.

The name Holly (f) comes either from the holly tree or from the word 'holy'. The third line of this prayer is a reference to Paul's letter to the Ephesians 3.17. For Hollie (f) see appendix.

Holy God, pour the sunshine and rain

Of your life-giving blessings on Holly;

Let her be rooted and grounded in your love;

Let her life be evergreen,

Yielding fruit as bright as berries.

The origins of the name Howard (m) are uncertain but it may come from Scandinavia, meaning 'high guardian' or from Germany, meaning 'heart protection'.

Harbour to the traveller, God give you haven,

Open sea after narrow straits, God speed your voyage,

Wind in the sails, God fill you with his Spirit,

Anchor in treacherous currents, God hold you safe,

Rudder beneath the waves, God guide your way,

Dawn after darkest night, God bring you light.

The name, Hunter (m), has the same meaning as its use in general vocabulary. It probably began as a surname and was adopted as a Christian name later. The fourth line of the prayer refers to Matthew 6.33.

Help Hunter, Lord, to use a hunter's skills –

Understanding a quarry's nature and ways,

Noticing signs, following tracks –

To seek and find the kingdom of God,

Even as you also seek him out to bless him,

Rescue him, and keep him in your love.

Ian and Iain (m) are Scottish versions of the name John. The prayer for Ian is based on Psalm 36.9 & John 6.35.

In God's light may you see light,

At God's well may you draw life,

Nourished by God, may you never be hungry.

In the name of the Father, a blessing of love,

A blessing of life, in the name of the Son,

In the name of the Spirit, a blessing of peace,

Now and always, your blessing from the Three.

The name Imogen (f) seems to have begun life as a misprint for the Celtic name Innogen (which may in turn come from the Gaelic for 'girl' or from the Latin for 'innocent'). When Shakespeare's play Cymbeline was printed the double 'nn' became an 'm'.

In all your days,

May God bless you;

On all your ways,

God go with you;

Even though you stray,

Never may God leave you.

Irene (f) comes from the Greek for 'peace' (from which we derive the word irenic).

In your heart, the peace of God

Refreshing your soul, the peace of God

Embracing you in love, the peace of God

Nurturing you in grace, the peace of God

Evermore and evermore, the peace of God.

Isaac (m) means 'laughter' in Hebrew. In the Bible Isaac was the son of Abraham and Sarah. Abraham was one hundred years old when Isaac was born and Sarah said, 'God has made laughter for me' (Genesis 21.6, RSV).

In the name of the Father of every blessing,

Seven blessings from God be upon you:

A blessing of laughter, of friendship and of joy,

A blessing of protection, of fulfilment and of peace,

Crowning all, the greatest blessing of love.

Isabel, Isobel, Isabella and Isabelle (all f) are forms of Elizabeth (from the Spanish, Italian and French). For Isabel and Isabella see appendix.

In your growing and your learning,

Spirit of God nurture you.

As you suffer and as you hurt,

Be the healing of God within you.

Every choice that you make,

Let the wisdom of God guide you.

Let the blessing of God go with you

Every journey you undertake.

In all that you undertake,

Spirit of God support you.

On each decision that you make,

Be the wisdom of God to guide you.

Every morning that you wake,

Let the blessing of God be with you.

Isaiah (m) means 'salvation of Yahweh' in Hebrew. Isaiah was a major prophet in the Old Testament appearing both as a character (2 Kings 19.2) and as the author of the book of Isaiah, famous for his prophecies of the coming Messiah (e.g. Isaiah 9.2–7) and message of hope (e.g. Isaiah 40.1–5).

In the mercy of God may you find

Salvation and forgiveness;

And may you know yourself beloved

In the infinite love of God;

And in God's grace may you receive

His blessings of light and joy and peace.

Isla (f) is derived from the Scottish island, Islay.

In the sea of God's love, like an island

Surrounded by the swell of God's tide,

Let the waves of God's blessings break upon you,

And wash your shores with his peace.

Originally a diminutive of John, Jack (m) has been the most popular name given to boys born in England and Wales every single year from 1994 to the most recent figures (2008). For Jackson (m) see appendix.

Joy be yours, and comfort in sadness,

Affection be yours, and the company of friends,

Courage be yours, and protection in danger,

Kindness be yours, from the King of all kings.

In the Bible Jacob (m) is the son of Isaac and Rebekah and twin brother of Esau. The Biblical account (Genesis 25.26) suggests the name means 'he takes by the heel' or 'supplanter' because Jacob came out of the womb holding his twin brother's heel and he later tricked him out of his inheritance. The Hebrew name Yaakov may also mean 'May God protect'.

Jesus defend and protect you

Against all danger and dismay;

Christ guide and direct you,

On the turnings of your way;

Bless you and keep you all your days.

Jacqueline (f) comes from the French and is a diminutive form of Jacques (the French equivalent of James).

Jesus be with you,

And grant you

Comfort in sorrow,

Quiet in conflict,

Understanding in perplexity,

Encouragement in despondency,

Light in darkness,

Innumerable blessings,

Never-ending love,

Eternal life.

Jake (m) is a diminutive of Jacob (which may mean 'God protect').

Just as you are, God bless you and take you,

As you could become, God nurture and make you,

Keep and protect you from all that would break you,

Even to eternity, never forsake you.

James (m) is a Biblical name sharing the same root as Jacob. The list of Jesus' twelve disciples includes James the brother of John and James the son of Alphaeus. James the brother of Jesus (Mark 6.3) became a leader of the early church (Galatians 2.9). The prayer for Jamie (m/f) is based on the Biblical prayer known as 'the grace' (2 Corinthians 13.14).

Jesus, bless James on his journey through life,

Almighty Father, assist him in all his adventures,

May your Spirit support and strengthen him

Everywhere he goes and in everything he does,

Safe in your care and sure of your love.

Jesus, grant you his grace,

And the Father his love,

May the fellowship of the Holy Spirit be with you,

In you, beside you, before you,

Evermore. Amen.

Jane (f) and all related names are derived from John (via the French Jeanne). For Jayne, Janet, Janine and Jan (all f) see appendix.

Jesus bless you with his risen life,

And keep you in his love;

Never-ending, unconditional love,

Everlasting, abundant life.

Jesus bless you with his life and light,

And keep you in his love and peace;

Never-ending, unconditional love,

Everlasting, abundant life,

The peace which this world cannot give,

The light which darkness cannot overcome,

Evermore and evermore.

Jesus bless you with his life and peace,

And keep you in his light and love;

Never-ending love,

Inextinguishable light,

Constant peace,

Everlasting life.

Jasmine (f) comes from the plant of the same name with small, fragrant white flowers.

Jesus Christ bless you,

And nurture you in his love;

So may your roots be deep and sustaining,

May your flowers be abundant and beautiful,

In fragrance rich and rare,

Never failing to flourish

Every year of your life.

Jason (m) derives from the Greek meaning 'to heal'. When Paul brought the gospel to Thessalonica he and his companions were hosted and protected by Jason, a convert and leader of the first church there (Acts 17.5–9).

Jesus bless you,

Always love you,

Sometimes surprise you,

Often inspire you,

Never leave you.

Jay (m/f) may originate as a shortened form of any name beginning with the letter J, and so this prayer incorporates four words with J as the initial letter. Alternatively Jay may be associated with the bird of the same name.

Jesus grant you joy and peace,

And journey every day beside you;

Your spirit be ever joined with his.

Jayden (m) comes from Jadon (mentioned in Nehemiah 3.7 as Nehemiah's helper in rebuilding the walls of Jerusalem). It comes from the Hebrew meaning either 'thankful' or 'Jehovah has heard'. For Jaden (m) see appendix.

Jesus be your help in need

And your friend to listen,

Your walls of defence in danger.

Deeply may he love you,

Eternally may he bless you,

Never may he forsake you.

Jean (f) comes (via the French) from John.

Jesus bless you with his risen life –

Everlasting, abundant life;

And God keep you in his love –

Never-ending, unconditional love.

Jeffrey (m) is a variant spelling of Geoffrey, from the old German meaning 'peace' or 'peaceful ruler'.

Jesus' blessings be

Ever upon you;

Forever may his love grow within you,

Forever may his peace flow upon you;

Rising every day, may he renew your hope,

Every night may he be

Your source of rest and refreshment.

Jemima (f) comes originally from the Hebrew meaning 'dove'. In the Bible we are told that Job named his eldest daughter Jemimah (Job 42.14–5) and there were no more beautiful women in the world than Jemimah and her sisters.

Jesus keep you

Eternally in his love.

May his peace dwell evermore

In the heart and soul of your being.

May his blessing be upon you

And remain with you always.

Jennifer (f) is a Cornish form of Guinevere (meaning 'white ghost'). For Jenna (f), Jennie (f) and Jenny (f) see appendix.

Jesus bless you,

Evermore love you,

Never leave you,

Nor forsake you,

In sadness comfort you,

From evil keep you,

Everywhere go with you

Right to the journey's end.

Jeremiah (m) is Hebrew for 'the Lord exalts' or 'appointed by the Lord'. Jeremiah is one of the great prophets in the Old Testament, ministering from 627 BC to around 580 BC. His words are recorded in the book of Jeremiah (and possibly Lamentations). Jeremy (m) and Jerry (m) are shortened forms of the name.

Jesus, risen Lord,

Equip and appoint Jeremiah to do your will,

Raise him with you from lamentation,

Exalt him with you to joy.

May your blessing be with him,

In him, around him,

Above him, below him,

Here and now, everywhere and always.

Jesus, risen Lord,

Equip and appoint Jeremy to do your will,

Raise him with you from lamentation,

Exalt him with you to joy.

May your love be ever within him,

Your blessing upon him forever.

Jesus bless you,

Enfold you in his love,

Reach out to you when you are in need,

Raise you when you fall;

Your life be filled with his peace.

Jesse (m) comes from the Hebrew meaning 'God exists'. In the Bible Jesse was the father of David (1 Samuel 16.9). Isaiah prophesied, 'There shall come forth a shoot from the stump of Jesse, and a branch shall grow out of his roots' (Is. 11.1, RSV). St. Paul identifies this shoot as Jesus (Romans 15.12). This prayer connects the image of Jesus as a new shoot with Jesus, the true vine (John 15).

Jesus, the true vine,

Engraft you to himself,

Sustain you through drought,

Support you through storm,

Enrich you with fruit.

Jessica (f) is derived from the Hebrew Iscah meaning 'God is looking'. Iscah was Abraham's niece (Genesis 11.29). For the shortened form of Jessie (f) see appendix.

Jesus, look on Jessica with your favour,

Encouraging her by your grace to be

Swift to share and care for those in need,

Slow to take offence or think ill of others.

In all her journey through life keep your

Constant watch over all her ways

And guide and protect her all her days.

Jill (f) probably derives from Julian.

Jesus bless you and dwell within you,

In your heart may his love make a home,

Let his peace abide in each room of your life,

Let his light shine forth from the windows of your soul.

The names Joan (f), Joanna (f) and Joanne (f) are feminine versions of John. Joanna, the wife of Chuza, is mentioned both as one of Jesus' followers (Luke 8.3) and as one of the very first witnesses of the resurrection (Luke 24.10). For Joanne see appendix.

Jesus bless you and walk with you

On every path of your journey,

And grant that by his guidance and protection

No trouble may ever overcome you.

Jesus bless you and walk with you

On every path of your journey,

And grant that by his guidance and protection

No temptation may ever lead you from the way

Nor any trouble ever overcome you

All the days of your life.

Joel (m) is a Hebrew name meaning 'Yahweh is God' (Yahweh being the holy name of God in the Old Testament). In the Bible Joel is a prophet and the author of a book by the same name.

Jesus' peace dwell deeply within you

On you may his light shine always brightly

Each day may his blessings flow freshly upon you

Let his love remain faithfully with you for ever.

John (m) comes from the Hebrew meaning 'God is merciful' or 'God is gracious'. In the Bible John the Baptist prepares the way for Jesus; another John is one of Jesus closest disciples; John is the author of the fourth gospel and three letters. The John who wrote the book of Revelation is probably a different author.

Journey on with God beside you,

Outwards through unknown lands, may he guide you,

Homewards, may he welcome and caress you,

Now and always may God bless you.

Jonathan (m) comes from the Hebrew meaning 'God has given'. Jonathan was the son of King Saul and faithful friend of David (1 Samuel 18.1–4).

Jesus, pour your blessings

On Jonathan:

Nourishment for the soul,

An appetite for all that is good,

Thirst for your love,

Hunger for justice,

And a place at your table

Now and in heaven.

The name Jordan (m/f) comes from the river in which Jesus was baptised (Mark 1.9) and which the Israelites crossed to enter the promised land (Joshua 3–4). Jordan is a Hebrew name meaning 'flowing down'. This prayer also draws upon Amos 5.24: 'Let justice roll down like waters, and righteousness like an ever-flowing stream' (RSV).

Justice and peace flow down upon you,

Over the fields of your spirit;

River of love and joy,

Deep river of God's blessings,

Always flow afresh upon you;

Never may that river run dry.

JOSEPH – *the good shepherd.*

Joseph (m) comes from the Hebrew meaning 'God has added' (this child). In the Old Testament Joseph was Jacob's favourite son (Genesis 3.22–50.26). In the New Testament Joseph was the husband of Mary, the mother of Jesus (Matthew 1.18–2.23). The prayer for Joseph is based on Psalm 23. José (m) is the Spanish equivalent of Joseph.

Jesus, good shepherd, lead Joseph

On paths of righteousness and through green pastures.

Stay close by to protect and comfort him as his path

Enters the valley of the shadow of death.

Provide for the refreshment of his soul so that,

Having you, he may lack nothing.

Jesus' blessing be in you and around you,

Over you and under you,

Everywhere and evermore.

Just as God chose Joseph to be the father

Of Jesus, our saviour and lord,

So may he bless you and choose you,

Employing you for some unique purpose.

Joshua (m) is a Hebrew name meaning 'God saves'. In the Bible Joshua succeeded Moses as leader of Israel (Deuteronomy 31). The book of Joshua tells how he brought the Israelites into the promised land.

Jesus, Saviour, grant that Joshua may be

Open and honest in all he does,

Safe in your shelter wherever he goes,

Healthy and happy in himself,

Unselfish and understanding towards others,

Always abiding in your love.

Joy (f) is named after the virtue. Joy is one of the nine fruits of the Spirit in Paul's letter to the Galatians (5.22–23). This prayer is also based upon Jesus' conversation with the woman at the well in Samaria (John 4.7–15).

Jesus' joy be a spring within you,

Offering water to quench your deepest thirst,

Yet never running dry.

Joyce (f) may derive from the Norman French meaning 'lord' but is now more naturally associated with the virtue 'joy'.

Jesus, give Joyce your peace,

On her may your blessings abound,

Your love find a home in her heart.

Christ Jesus, fill her life with your joy,

Even as you rejoice in her love.

Judith (f) comes from the Hebrew meaning a woman of Judea. In the Bible the book of Judith is to be found in the apocrypha – the story of a beautiful and faithful widow who saved the Jews from Assyrian punishment. For Judy (f) see appendix.

Jesus' blessing be upon you,

Under you God's everlasting arms,

Deep within you the Spirit of peace.

In your heart may Jesus' love abide,

The protection of God surround you,

His Holy Spirit fill you with joy.

Julia (f) and all its variations come from the Roman family name Julius (itself meaning possibly 'downy' or 'soft-haired' from the Greek). For Julian (m), Julie (f) and Juliet (f) see appendix.

Joy from God's laughter be with you,

Understanding from God's word guide you,

Love from God's heart embrace you,

Inner peace from God's spirit fill you,

And blessings of God's grace be upon you.

Joy from God's laughter be with you,

Understanding from God's word guide you,

Love from God's heart embrace you,

Inner peace from God's spirit fill you,

Energy from God's life abound in you.

The strength of God's arm protect you,

The blessings of God's grace be upon you,

Evermore and evermore.

Justin (m) and Justine (f) come from the Latin meaning 'just', 'fair' or 'righteous'. This prayer is based on Isaiah 1.17. For Justin omit the last line.

Jesus bless you and inspire you to

Uphold the weak,

Seek justice,

Try to do good,

Intercede for those in need;

Nurturing you in his loving care,

Every day of your life.

Kai (m) has many possible meanings in different languages, but the meaning 'keeper of keys' (from Scandinavian languages) is incorporated in this prayer.

Keeper of heaven's keys, keep Kai in your love,

And open for him the lock

In the door to your store of blessings.

Kaitlin (f) is a variant spelling of Caitlin, an Irish form of Katherine which may derive from the Greek *katharos* meaning 'pure'. The fifth and sixth lines refer to Zechariah 13.9. For Katelyn (f) see appendix.

King of heaven bless you

And keep you pure in heart

In every trial and temptation.

The Lord God grant you perfect peace,

Like silver refined of all impurity

In the fire of his love,

Now and always. Amen.

Karen (f) comes from the Danish form of Catherine. The opening verb here echoes 1 Samuel 18.1 ('The soul of Jonathan was knit to the soul of David, and Jonathan loved him as his own soul' RSV) and Psalm 86.11: 'O knit my heart unto thee' (Book of Common Prayer).

Knit your Spirit to Karen's spirit,

And love her, Lord, as your own soul;

Reside forever within her heart,

Enfold her years within your eternity,

Now and always splice her being with blessings.

Katherine (f) may be derived from the Greek *katharos* meaning 'pure'. The second line refers to Isaiah 26.3 and the fourth to Deuteronomy 33.27. For Katharine (f) and Kathryn (f) see appendix.

King of peace bless you

And keep you in perfect peace;

The God of love bless you,

Hold you in his everlasting arms;

Eternal Father bless you,

Remain with you always;

Inextinguishable Light bless you,

Now and always guide you,

Evermore shine upon you.

Katie (f) and Kitty (f) are diminutives of Katherine. For Kate (f) omit the fourth line of Katie.

Keep Katie in your love, O Lord,

And keep her happy and healthy;

Through times of danger keep her safe,

In her way through life keep her on the right path;

Every day bless her and keep her.

Kind and caring God,

Immerse Kitty in your love

Today and every day,

That she may be safe in your blessing,

Year after year, forever.

Kathleen (f) is an Anglicised version of the Irish Caitlin, which is ultimately derived from Katharine.

King of peace bless you

And keep you in perfect peace;

The God of love bless you,

Hold you in his everlasting arms;

Lord of all hopefulness bless you,

Encourage and inspire you;

Everlasting Light bless you,

Now and always shine upon you.

Katrina (f) is a Scottish variation of Katharine (possibly via the Italian Catriona).

Kindness of God's love be always with you

Assistance of God's angels be always with you

Tenderness of God's peace be always with you

Radiance of God's light be always with you

Inspiration of God's word be always with you

Nearness of God's Spirit be always with you

Abundance of God's life be always with you.

KAYLA – *let her enter the narrow gate.*

Kayla and Kayleigh (f) probably derive via Kelly (f/m) from the Irish *caol* meaning 'narrow' or 'slender'. These prayers refer to Jesus' direction, 'Enter by the narrow gate … for the gate is narrow and the way is hard, that leads to life' (Matthew 7.13–14, RSV). For Kaylee (f) see appendix.

Kindly Lord, bless Kayla

And by your strength,

Your grace and your guidance,

Let her enter the narrow gate,

And follow the hard road leading to life.

Kindly Lord, bless Kayleigh

And by your strength,

Your grace and your guidance,

Let her find the narrow gate,

Enter and follow the hard road

In the way that leads to life:

God bless her and love her,

Help her and keep her always.

Kindly Lord, grant Kelly

Every blessing and guidance;

Let her enter by the narrow gate,

Let her follow the road which is hard

Yet which leads to your eternal life.

Keira (f) means 'little dark-haired one'. The first line of this prayer plays upon the sound of the opening syllable of the name.

Key to life's mystery, open your blessings to Keira,

Energy of life, pour your blessings on her,

Infinite love, embrace her with your blessings,

Radiant light, shine your blessings upon her,

Abundant life, fill her with your blessings.

Keith (m) comes from the Gaelic meaning 'forest' or 'wood' or 'windy place'.

Keeper of souls, keep Keith

Evermore in your love,

In your peace and your joy.

Touch him gently with your blessings,

Hold him safely in your arms.

Kenneth (m) comes from the Gaelic meaning 'fire-born' or 'handsome'. This prayer explores the image of fire, drawing on phrases from Charles Wesley's hymn, 'O thou who camest from above'.

Kindle in Kenneth a spark of your life, Lord,

Embers of your sacred love stir up into flame.

Nurture within him the fire of your Spirit;

Never let storm or tempest

Extinguish the blaze of your hope.

Tend your light within Kenneth, Lord;

Holy Spirit, let it shine.

The name, Kevin (m), comes from Ireland and means 'comely' or 'fair'.

Keep your watch of love over Kevin, Lord,

Encircle him with your strong defence,

Vanquish every evil that threatens him,

Increase in him every good desire,

Now and always bless him, Lord.

Kian (m) comes from the Irish meaning 'ancient', which suggested the divine name 'Ancient of Days' (Daniel 7.9,13,22). The two other names for God used in the prayer come from 1 Timothy 6.15 and from J.G. Whittier's hymn, 'Immortal love, for ever full'.

King of Kings, give Kian your peace,

Immortal Love, fill his heart with your grace,

Ancient of Days, bless the years which lie before him,

Now and always, keep him in eternal life.

Kieran (m) means 'little dark-haired one'. The first line of this prayer plays upon the sound of the opening syllable of the name. For Kieron (m) see appendix.

Key to life's mystery, open your blessings to Kieran,

Infinite love of life, embrace him with your blessings,

Energy of life, pour your blessings over him,

Radiant light of life, shine your blessings upon him,

Abundant life, fill him with your blessings,

Newness of life, bless him afresh each day.

Kimberley (f/m) comes originally from an old English place name meaning 'Cyneburga's wood' but came into use as a Christian name after the relief of the siege of Kimberley in South Africa during the Boer War. For Kimberly (f/m) see appendix.

King of peace, pour your peace

Into the cup of Kimberley's soul.

Maker and care-taker of all that is,

Bless her and keep her in your care.

Everlasting light, stronger than darkness,

Radiate upon her your life-giving light.

Love divine, stronger than death,

Embrace her and grant her

Your love and life eternal.

Kirsty (f) is a Scottish diminutive of Christine.

Keep Kirsty constantly

In your love, Lord;

Raise her up

Safely when she falls;

Touch her gently with

Your blessings of peace.

Kylie (f) probably derives (via Kelly) from the Irish *caol* meaning 'narrow' or 'slender'. This prayer refers to Jesus' direction, 'Enter by the narrow gate … for the gate is narrow and the way is hard, that leads to life' (Matthew 7.13–14, RSV). For Kyle (m/f) see appendix.

Kindly Lord, grant Kylie

Your blessing and your guidance:

Let her find and follow

In the way that leads to life,

Even though the road may be hard and the gate narrow.

Lacey (f) derives from the place name Lassy in Normandy but is also often associated with decorative lace.

Let your life be a richly woven tapestry,

And every thread a grace of God:

Crafted with his care, laced with his love,

Embroidered with joy, knit together with peace,

Your life be shot through with his blessings.

Lachlan (m) comes from the Gaelic meaning 'land of the lakes'. Originally from Scotland, the name is especially popular in Australia and Canada.

Let the love of Christ enfold you,

As deep as the loch's deep waters.

Christ's blessing be upon you,

High as the mountain peaks above.

Let the peace of Christ support you,

As sure as the ground beneath your feet,

Now and always. Amen.

Lara (f) is a diminutive form of Larissa.

Lasting be your joys

And fleeting be your sorrows;

Rich be God's blessings upon you

And endless be his love.

Laura (f) is named after the laurel plant. Crowns of laurel leaves were given to victorious athletes in Roman games, or leaders of triumphant armies. Laurence (m), also spelled Lawrence (m), comes from the Roman town Laurentium, which meant a place of laurels. For Lauren (f), Laurence, Laurie and Lawrie (all m) see appendix.

Loving Lord, may you be

Above Laura to watch over her

Under her to support her

Round her to protect her

Always with her to bless her.

Let the love of God be

Above you to watch over you

Within you to strengthen you

Round you to protect you

Encircling you to embrace you

Near you to comfort you.

Christ bless you and keep you

Everywhere and evermore.

Layla (f) comes from the Arabic meaning 'night', 'beauty', 'dark', or 'wine'.

Lord, let your love embrace Layla as surely

As the night enfolds the world in its darkness,

Your peace be to her as deep as a dreamless sleep,

Let your blessings upon her be as numerous

As the stars above in the clear night sky.

Leah (f) was the older sister of Rachel, both of whom were wives to Jacob (Genesis 29.1–30). The name comes from the Hebrew meaning 'weary'. This prayer is also based on words from Isaiah 40.28–31.

Let the God who never grows weary,

Empower you when you are faint,

And when you are weary raise you up

Higher than the wings of soaring eagles.

Lee (m/f) comes from the Old English meaning a 'field', 'meadow', 'clearing' or 'wood'.

Let everything you do be blessed with God's grace,

Every part of you be filled with his love,

Every day of your life be graced by his blessing.

Leo (m) comes from the Latin for 'lion'. For Leon (m) see appendix.

Let all your strength be drawn from God,

Every path you take be guided by God,

On all your days be the blessings of God.

———————

Lesley (f) and Leslie (m) are Scottish in origin, possibly from a place name meaning 'a garden by water'.

Let the love of God bless you,

Even as you

Seek to love and serve others.

Let the peace of God fill you,

Even as you give others

Your peace and your blessing.

Let God bless you with love,

Even as you

Seek to love and bless others.

Let God pour his peace

Into your heart,

Even as you give peace to others.

Lewis (m) is an Anglicised form of Louis.

Look after Lewis, with your loving protection,

Every day and everywhere,

While awake and while asleep,

In weakness and in strength,

Shepherd and shield of our souls.

———————

Lexie (f) is a shortened form of Alexandra. For Lexi (f) see appendix.

Let God turn your troubles to blessings,

Endings to beginnings,

eXchange your disappointment for hope,

In place of anxiety may he give you peace,

Every sorrow may he transform into joy.

———————

Liam (m) is a shortened form of William. Liam is derived from the old German 'helm' meaning protection.

Let the love of God protect you

In body, mind and spirit;

And in all you do and wherever you go

May the blessing of God go with you.

Libby (f) began as a shortened form of Elizabeth or Olivia.

Let the blessings of God be always

In you, with you and upon you;

Blessings of peace, blessings of joy,

Blessings of love from the God of life,

Your maker, provider, sustainer.

Lily (f) is one of many flower names. Lilies are symbolic of purity and are often associated with Mary the mother of Jesus. For Lilly and Lillian (f) see appendix.

Lord, grant Lily your love, peace and purity,

In all she thinks and says and does.

Let her remain always in your protection,

Your guidance and your care.

Linda (f) is a shortened form of Belinda. For Lynda (f) see appendix.

Let the love of God be in your heart,

In your thinking and speaking, his mercy,

Newness of life in your spirit,

Deep peace in all you do,

And the blessing of God be always with you.

Lindsay & Lindsey (f/m) come originally from a place name in Lincolnshire meaning 'island of Lincoln' or 'island of Linden trees'. For Lyndsay (f/m) see appendix.

Let the blessing of God be with you,

In you, around you, above you, before you;

Night by night, God replenish your rest,

Day by day, your hope;

Second by second, God keep you in his care,

And hour by hour, in his peace,

Year after year in his love.

Let the blessing of God be with you,

In you, around you, above you, before you;

Night by night, God replenish your rest,

Day by day, your hope;

So may each moment be filled with God's grace,

Each matter with peace, each meeting with love,

Year after year for evermore.

The name Lisa (f) developed as a shortened form of Elizabeth.

Let the strong arms of God enfold you

In his loving embrace,

Support you when you are weary,

And protect you from all harm.

Logan (m) is a Scottish place name, possibly meaning a 'hollow'.

Let God's blessing be to you an

Oasis in the wilderness,

Gateway to new life,

A lantern to your feet,

Nourishment for your soul.

Lola (f) comes from the Spanish *dolores* meaning sorrows (from Maria de los Dolores – Mary of the Sorrows).

Let your sorrows be seldom and short,

Often and long your joys;

Let God's blessing on you be always,

And his love for you be forever.

The name Lorna (f) seems to have been invented by the author R. D. Blackmore for his novel *Lorna Doone* (1896).

Long be your joys and short your sorrows,

Often your laughter and few your tears,

Rich God's gifts to you, deep his peace,

New his hope and numerous his blessings,

Abundant his life and forever his love.

Lorraine (f) comes from the name of the region in the North East of France. The second line of this prayer quotes from Romans 6.9.

Let the risen Lord Jesus,

Over whom death has no more dominion,

Raise you from sorrow to joy,

Raise you from turmoil to peace,

After disappointment raise you to hope,

In darkness raise you to light,

Now and always bless you,

Evermore raise you to new life.

Louise (f) and Louisa (f) are derived from the German name Ludwig meaning 'famous warrior'. Luisa (f), Louis (m), Louie (m), and Luis (m) can all be formed by omitting lines from the names below.

Let God's blessing be

Over you to guide you,

Under you to carry you,

In you to inspire you,

Surrounding you to shield you,

Embracing you to love you.

Let God's blessing be

Over you to guide you,

Under you to carry you,

In you to inspire you,

Surrounding you to shield you,

Ahead of you to lead you.

Lucas (m) and Luca (m) are variant forms of Luke. Lucas comes from the Latin and appeared in this form in early English translations of the New Testament. Luca is from the Italian. For Luca see appendix.

Look with your gracious favour, Lord,

Upon Lucas and pour upon him

Countless blessings, your perfect peace,

Abundant life which comes only from you,

Source of all love and goodness.

Lucy (f) and Lucinda (f) are derived from the Latin *lux* meaning 'light'. Jesus said, 'I am the light of the world' (John 8.12).

Let the light of God's life,

Understanding, guidance and truth,

Cast away all darkness from around you,

Illuminate the path before you,

Nurture you in the warmth of his love,

Dazzle you with a glimpse of his glory,

And shine his blessings upon you.

Let the light of God's life and love,

Understanding, guidance and truth,

Cast away all darkness and shine upon you,

Your family and all you love.

Luke (m) was the author of the third gospel and probably also the book of Acts. He was a companion of Paul on his journeys and is referred to by Paul as 'the beloved physician' (Colossians 4.14). As a result Luke is associated with healing and doctors.

Look with favour, Lord, on Luke,

Unique in his own special gifts and character.

Keep him safe in your nurturing love,

Every day of his life.

Lydia (f) is a region in Asia Minor and when given to a person the name originally meant a woman from this place. One of Paul's converts at Philippi is called Lydia (Acts 16.14–15).

Let your blessings reside in Lydia, Lord,

Your love make a home in her heart;

Dwell in her soul, Spirit of God;

Inhabit her mind, wisdom of God;

Abide in her always, peace of God.

Lyn, Lynn and Lynne (all f/m) began as shortened forms of names such as Llewelyn, Lindsay or Linda, but they have become names in their own right. For Lynn omit the last line of Lynne.

Let your heart be filled with God's love,

Your spirit be filled with his peace;

Night and day, your life be filled with his blessings.

Let your heart be filled with God's love,

Your spirit be filled with his peace;

Nowhere you go be beyond his protection,

Nothing you do be lacking his grace,

Evermore may you be filled with his blessings.

Lysbeth (f) is a variant form of Elizabeth.

Look upon Lysbeth with

Your loving kindness, Lord:

Support her with your strength;

Bless her with your grace;

Encourage her with your hope;

Tend her with your comfort,

Heal her with your peace.

Mackenzie (f/m) is a Scottish clan name meaning 'son of Kenneth'. In Canada it is also associated with the Mackenzie River.

May the life of God

Abound within you;

Compassion of God

Keep you in his love;

Each day God's daily bread

Nourish and sustain you;

Zeal of God for all things good

Inspire you and encourage you;

Evermore may God bless you.

Maddison (f) derives either from 'the son of Maud' or from 'Magdalene' as in Mary Magdalene (Luke 8.2). This prayer is based upon phrases from the Lord's Prayer (Matthew 6.9–13). For Madison (f) see appendix.

May the Son of God bless you,

And forgive you as you forgive others,

Daily feed you in body and soul,

Deliver you from evil,

In times of temptation

Strengthen you to do his will

On earth, as it is in heaven,

Now and forever. Amen.

Madeleine (f) and Madeline (f) are derived from Magdalene, meaning 'from Magdala' – a town on the Sea of Galilee. Mary Magdalene was the first to find the empty tomb and meet the risen Jesus (John 20.1–18). For Madeline omit the sixth line.

May God endow you with grace,

And enkindle his fire within you,

Develop and encourage you,

Enhance your enjoyment of life.

Let the love of God enfold you,

Enlighten your way in the darkness,

In danger encircle you,

Nourish and enrich you,

Evermore, love without end.

Maisie (f) was originally a shortened form of Margaret.

May God bless you

And keep you

In his perfect peace,

Surround you

In his strong protection,

Enfold you in his love.

Makayla (f) and Mikayla (f) are variations of Michaela (f). The last line echoes John 15.11. For Mikayla and Michaela see appendix.

May the blessings of God,

Around you and within you,

Keep you in perfect peace;

And by God's grace may

Your heart be content,

Let your hopes be fulfilled,

And your joy be complete.

The name Mala (f) derives from Magdalene (as in Mary Magdalene). This prayer is based on the Aaronic blessing (Numbers 6.24–26).

May God bless you and watch over you,

And make his face to shine upon you;

Let the Lord look kindly on you,

And give you peace.

Malcolm (m) comes from the Gaelic meaning 'a disciple of [St.] Columba'. Columba itself means 'dove'.

May God's love come upon you,

As his Son came down to earth at Christmas.

Let God's peace come upon you, as the Spirit

Came down in the form of a dove

On Jesus at his baptism.

Like the gifts of the Spirit which came at Pentecost,

May God's blessings be ever upon you.

Marcus (m) is the Latin form of Mark. Both Marcus and Marcia (f) may derive from the Roman name Marcius (which itself is linked to Mars, the God of war). For Marcia see appendix.

Morning by morning God renew your hope

And evening by evening God restore your peace

Round you and within you God protect you

Constantly and unconditionally God love you

Until the end of time God be with you

So may God's blessings be forever upon you.

Margaret (f) and Marjorie (f) come from the Greek *margaron* meaning 'pearl'. For Margery (f) see appendix.

May God bless you

And keep you in his love,

Reach out to you in need,

Grant you his peace;

And may God look kindly on you,

Refresh your soul when you are weary,

Embrace you when you are sad,

Today and all your days.

May God bless you

And enfold you in his love,

Reach out to you in your need,

Journey beside you through life.

Over you may God keep his watch,

Round you may God set his guard,

In your heart may God abide,

Evermore may God grant you peace.

Maria (f) and its variations are all derived from Mary. These prayers are based upon words which the angel spoke to Mary (Luke 1.28 & 30), and which she spoke in the song known as the 'magnificat' (Luke 1.48 & 49). For Mair, Mariah, Marian, Marianne, Marie and Marion (all f) see appendix.

May the Lord be with you

And do great things for you,

Regarding your lowliness with his favour.

In his graciousness may he bless you

And fill you with his love.

May the Lord be with you

And find favour with you,

Richly blessing you

In love and joy and peace,

Looking upon your lowliness

Yet doing great things for you

Now and always.

The name Mark (m) comes originally from the Roman God, Mars. In the book of Acts, John Mark is a companion of Paul (Acts 12.25). The gospel according to Mark is widely considered to be the first gospel to be written. This prayer refers to Genesis 4.15: when Cain was sent out to wander the earth, the Lord put his mark on him to protect him.

May the Lord bless you

And place his mark of love upon you,

Rescuing you from every danger,

Keeping you in his perfect peace.

Martha (f), comes from the Aramaic meaning 'lady.' In the Bible Martha was one of Jesus' close friends and the sister of Mary (Luke 10.38–42, John 11.1–44, 12.2). This prayer is based on an old Irish blessing.

May the road rise to meet you

And the wind be always at your back,

Rain fall softly on your fields,

The sun shine warm upon your face;

He who holds the universe, hold you

And keep you safe in the palm of his hand.

Martin (m) probably comes originally from Mars, the Roman god of war. This prayer, like Martha's, is based upon an old Irish blessing.

May the road rise to meet you

And the wind be always at your back,

Rain fall softly on your fields,

The sun shine warm upon your face;

In the name of God who holds you

Now and always in the palm of his hand.

There are several women called Mary (f) in the New Testament, the first and foremost being Jesus' mother. This prayer is based upon words which the angel spoke to her (Luke 1.28 & 30), and which she spoke in the song known as the 'magnificat' (Luke 1.48 & 49). For Mair (the Welsh form of Mary) & Maryam (f) see appendix.

May the Lord be with you

And find favour with you,

Regarding your lowliness

Yet doing great things for you.

Mason (m) is an occupational name, meaning one who worked or built with stone. This prayer is based on Jesus' parable of the two builders (Matthew 7.24–27).

> **M**ay the Son of God be your cornerstone,
>
> **A**nd your house be built on his rock;
>
> **S**o when storms arise and troubles come,
>
> **O**n God's foundations you will stand firm,
>
> **N**othing will overcome you.

Matilda (f) comes from the German meaning 'mighty in battle' or 'heroine'.

> **M**ay the God of hope bless you
>
> **A**t your waking and your rising,
>
> **T**he God of love sustain you
>
> **I**n your working and your journeying,
>
> **L**et the God of peace refresh you
>
> **D**uring your hours of rest and sleeping,
>
> **A**ll the days and years of your life.

Matthew (m) comes from the Hebrew meaning 'gift from God'. Matthew was a tax collector and became one of Jesus' twelve disciples (Matthew 9.9). The gospel according to Matthew is also attributed to his authorship.

May God's love and protection

Always go with you

Through trial and triumph,

Through trouble and thanksgiving,

Helping and holding,

Enabling and encouraging,

Wherever the path of life takes you.

Maureen (f) is an Anglicized version of the Irish Mairin which means 'little Mary'. This prayer draws on phrases from the service of Compline and Psalm 91.

May the Lord God keep you

As the apple of his eye;

Under the shadow of his wings may you find

Refuge and warmth for your soul.

Early in the morning may God bless your rising,

Evening by evening may he bless your resting,

Now and always may he preserve you in peace.

Max (m) is a shortened version either of Maximilian, meaning 'the greatest' (from the Latin *maximus*), or of Maxwell.

May Max be blessed with true greatness, Lord,

Ambitious to do your will,

e**X**celling in service of others.

Maxwell (m) is of Scottish origin meaning either 'Magnus' well' or 'large spring'. This prayer paraphrases Jesus' words to the Samaritan woman at the well (John 4.14).

May God become for you

A well-spring of living water,

e**X**isting deep within your soul,

Welling up within you,

Even to eternal life.

Let love, peace and joy be ever within you;

Let the blessing of God be ever upon you.

May (f) is named after the fifth month, a time of late spring.

May your young shoots grow under God's protection,

And your buds unfurl in God's light,

Your blossoms open to the warmth of God's love.

Maya (f) may either be related to the name Mary or may derive from Maia the Roman earth goddess of spring, after whom the month of May is named. For Maia (f) see appendix.

May God be to you a warm summer sun,

And the autumn harvest within you,

Your shelter when the winter storms come,

And a springtime of hope and new life.

Megan (f) is a Welsh pet-form of Margaret.

Maker of the miracle of each new life,

Encircle Megan with your love and protection,

Grant her your grace each day as she grows,

And guide and guard her wherever she goes,

Now and always. Amen.

MELISSA – *meaning honey bee.*

Melanie (f) means 'dark' (from the Greek *melas*) and was originally a name given to children with dark eyes or hair or complexion.

May the light of Christ shine

Eternally upon you;

Let the peace of God be

Always surrounding you;

Now may the love of God abide

In your heart and soul and mind,

Evermore and evermore.

Melissa (f) comes from the Greek meaning 'honey bee'.

May God keep you in his love

Each day of your life;

Let God pour his peace

Into the depths of your being;

Such peace as this world cannot give,

Such love as hopes and endures all things:

And may God bless you evermore.

Mia (f) comes either from Maria or from the Spanish or Italian for 'mine'.

May all that is mine be yours, O Lord,

In order that

All that is yours may be mine.

———————————

Michael (m) comes from the Hebrew meaning 'Who is like God?' In the Bible Michael is one of the archangels (Revelation 12.7). The prayers for Michael and Michelle (f) are based on St. Paul's wonderful passage about the nature of love (1 Corinthians 13). For Michaela (f) see appendix.

May God bless you and

Increase in you the gift of love:

Constant love that is patient and kind,

Healing love that bears and hopes all things,

Attentive love that puts others first,

Enriching love that overflows to all around you,

Love that endures and never ends.

May God bless you and

Increase in you the gift of love:

Constant love that is patient and kind,

Healing love that forgives and reconciles,

Enriching love that overflows to all around you,

Love that bears and hopes all things,

Love that endures all things,

Eternal love that never ends.

Millie (f) is short for Millicent or Amelia and is derived from the German for 'strong worker'.

May your blessing be on Millie, Lord,

In everything she does:

Let her working bring fulfilment;

Let her loving bring contentment;

In her going be her guide,

Each day walking by her side.

Molly (f) is a diminutive of Mary. For Mollie (f) see appendix.

Many the gifts of God to you:

Often the laughter, much the joy,

Little the sadness, short the trouble,

Long the friendships, deep the love,

Yours the blessings of God for ever.

The origins of the name Monica (f) are unknown. St. Monica (332–87) was the influential mother of Augustine of Hippo. This prayer is based upon Jesus' saying, 'I am the way' (John 14.6). In the early years of the Church, Christianity was known as 'the Way' (Acts 9.2 & 24.14).

May Jesus, who is himself the true way, bless you;

Open a new way when your path is closed;

Navigate your way when your path is lost;

Illuminate your way when you cannot see;

Carry you on the way when you cannot go on;

Accompany you on the way to your journey's end.

Morgan (f/m) is of Celtic origin, meaning either 'circling sea' or 'great brightness'. The second half of this prayer refers to Psalm 139.11–12.

May God guide you safely

Over every circling sea,

Round every dangerous cape.

God keep you in his great brightness,

As with God the darkness is no darkness;

Night is as clear as the day.

Muireann (f) is an Irish Gaelic name meaning 'sea fair'.

May God be with you on the sea of life,

Under your boat may the waves be gentle,

In stormy waters may God keep you safe,

Refresh you when your voyage is long,

Everywhere you go may God guide you,

Across wide oceans may God sustain you,

Near and far may God remain with you,

Now and always may God bless you.

Muriel (f) comes from the old Irish meaning 'sea bright'.

May God keep you in his blessings

Until the end of time,

Retain you in his peace

In the midst of every trouble;

Even though all else may pass away,

Let God's love remain with you forever.

Nancy (f) is a familiar form of Ann, meaning 'grace' in Hebrew.

Never may God deny you his help,

Always may God defend you;

Never may God depart from you,

Constantly may God love you;

Your life be blessed forever.

Natalie (f) comes from the Latin meaning 'birthday of the Lord' and in the past was given to girls born at Christmas time. The nativity of Jesus reminds us that he was flesh and blood, like us, and knew from the inside what it is to be human. Natasha (f) is a Russian form of Natalie.

Nativity child, crucified man, risen Lord,

As you shared the growing and the loving,

The pain and the passion of human life,

Accept Natalie with understanding and love;

Let your blessing be with her always;

In your compassion, share her suffering,

Even as she shares the joy of your risen life.

Nativity child, crucified man, risen Lord,

As you shared the growing and the loving,

The pain and the passion of human life,

Accept Natasha with compassion and love,

Share the burden of her suffering,

Help her in her times of need,

And bless her always with your peace.

Nathan and Nathaniel (m) are Biblical names, meaning 'gift' and 'gift of God'. Nathan was a prophet in the court of King David (2 Samuel 7). Nathanael (spelled like this in the Bible though now more usually with an 'i') was one of Jesus' disciples (John 1.45–50).

Never leave Nathan, Lord, wherever he goes,

Always assist him whatever he does;

Turn his trials to triumphs,

His hurts to healing,

Anxieties to adventures,

Needs to opportunities.

Never leave Nathaniel, Lord, wherever he goes,

Always assist him whatever he does;

Turn his trials to triumphs,

His hurts to healing,

Anxieties to adventures,

Needs to opportunities,

Ideals to action,

Exploration to discovery;

Let your blessing be with him for ever.

Neil (m) is from the Gaelic, meaning 'champion'.

Now and evermore may God bless you,

Evermore and everywhere may God guide you,

Into truth and into peace may God lead you,

Lovingly and graciously may God keep you.

The name Nevaeh (f) is formed from the letters of 'heaven' in reverse order.

Never forsake Nevaeh, Lord,

Ever guard and protect her,

Vouchsafe to bless her

And keep her in your love,

Even until you bring her

Home with you to heaven.

The Irish Gaelic Niamh (f), and its English spelling Neve (f), means 'bright'. The ending of Neve's prayer comes from Matthew 28.20.

Nurturing God, bless Niamh's beginning,

In her infancy may she grow in your grace,

As an adult may she use your gifts generously,

May she reach maturity fulfilled and happy,

Held in your love all the days of her life.

Never leave Neve, Lord,

Even to the ends of the earth;

Vouchsafe to love and look after her always,

Even to the very end of time.

Nicholas (m) and Nicola (f) come from the Greek meaning 'victory of the people'. St. Nicholas was Bishop of Myra in the 4th century. Legends of his shyness, his acts of generosity and patronage of children live on in the story and traditions surrounding Santa Claus. For Nicole (f) see appendix.

Now and always, God bless you,

In sickness and in health, God be with you,

Coming in and going out, God watch over you,

Hungry and thirsty, God feed you,

Outwardly and inwardly, God guide you,

Lost and found, God embrace you,

At work and at rest, God fulfil you,

Sleeping and waking, God love you.

Now and always, God bless you,

In sickness and in health, God be with you,

Coming in and going out, God watch over you,

Outwardly and inwardly, God guide you,

Lost and found, God embrace you,

Asleep and awake, God give you peace.

Nigel (m) comes from the Latin version of Neil.

Now and evermore may God be with you,

In his peace and love may God keep you,

Graciously and faithfully may God love you,

Everywhere and always may God guide you,

Lovingly and greatly may God bless you.

Nina (f) comes either from the Spanish for 'little girl' or from the Russian pet-form of Anne. This prayer is based on words by Teresa of Avila, the Spanish Carmelite nun and mystic (1515–82).

Nothing disturb you, nothing dismay you;

In God's love you can lack nothing.

Nothing discourage you, nothing defeat you;

All things pass, but God bless you always.

Noah (m) is from the Hebrew meaning 'rest', 'comfort' or 'long-lived'. The Biblical story of Noah and the ark is one of the best known stories in the Old Testament (Genesis chapters 6–9).

Now may the blessing of God be upon you,

Over you may his rainbow shine the promise of peace,

And may he bring you through storm and through flood,

Holding you safe in the ark of his love.

Norman (m) means 'north-man'. It was first applied to the Vikings and was well established as a name in England before the Norman conquest. For Norma (f) omit the last line.

Neither may evil harm you nor malice

Overcome you, but may God always

Rescue you and raise you up.

May the peace and the love and the joy

And the blessings of God be with you

Now and for all eternity. Amen.

OLIVIA – *from the olive tree and its fruit.*

Although similar, Oliver (m) and Olivia (f) probably come from different roots; Oliver from the Scandinavian Olaf meaning 'ancestor' and Olivia from the olive tree and its fruit. For Olive (f) see appendix.

On all that Oliver is and does,

Lord, grant your love and blessing.

In all the challenges he undertakes

Various gifts bestow upon him.

Everyone he loves and all who love him,

Reach out, Lord, to bless them through him.

Over your waking and going out

Let God keep watch and guard you.

In your making and your working

Various gifts of God equip you.

In your coming in and resting

All God's peace and love be with you.

Oscar (m) comes from the Gaelic and may mean 'gentle friend' or 'god-spear'.

Oldest and gentlest friend, dear God,

Stand by Oscar when he is in need,

Cheer him when he is sad,

Accompany him on his journey through life,

Rejoice with him when he is glad.

Owen (m) is a Welsh name, possibly meaning 'lamb'.

On each waking, God give you his blessing

Whatever your work, God give you fulfilment

Evening and night-time, God give you rest

Now and always, God give you his love.

Paige (f) means 'page' or 'servant'.

Peace be within you, though troubles surround you,

A spirit of service, though others serve themselves,

In your heart God's love, though you may feel unworthy,

God bless you and be with you always,

Even though time itself may cease.

The name Pamela (f) was invented by Sir Philip Sidney for his poem *Arcadia* (1590). He seems to have intended the meaning 'all sweetness' from the combination of Greek words for 'all' and 'honey'. The name became popular following the success of Samuel Richardson's novel *Pamela* (1740).

Permeate Pamela's soul, Lord,

And suffuse her spirit with peace.

May her heart be steeped in your love,

Each day be blended with blessings.

Let your hope sweeten every sorrow,

And your grace interlace every joy.

Patrick (m) and Patricia (f) derive from the Latin *patricius*, meaning 'of noble birth.' St. Patrick (c. 390–461) is credited with bringing Christianity to Ireland, where he is the patron saint. These prayers are based upon phrases from the ancient prayer known as 'St. Patrick's breastplate'.

Praise to the Three and praise to the One,

And invocation to the powers of heaven,

To bind around you the strong name of God,

Restoring you, comforting, shielding and blessing.

In quiet, in danger, Christ beside you,

Christ behind you, before you, within you,

In friend, in stranger, in those who love you,

Above you, beneath you, Christ be with you.

Praise to the Three and praise to the One,

And invocation to the powers of heaven,

To bind around you the strong name of God,

Restoring you, comforting, shielding and blessing.

In quiet, in danger, Christ beside you,

Christ behind you, before you, within you,

King of creation, Christ be with you.

This short prayer is based on words of St. Augustine of Hippo.

Place all that has been in the hands of God's mercy,

And entrust all that is, to his infinite love,

Then the blessing of God will provide for you always.

Paul (m) comes from the Latin meaning 'little'. St. Paul (died c. 65 AD) converted from being a persecutor of Christians to a great Christian missionary, apostle to the Gentiles and author of many New Testament letters which have profoundly influenced Christian theology. Paula (f) and Pauline (f) are feminine versions of Paul. The prayer for Paula offers an alternative prayer which could be interchanged with Paul by moving the Amen.

Powerful and gentle God, bless Paul,

And through your constant care let him

Understand that though he may be

Little in the world, he is great in your love.

Perfect peace from the God of peace to you,

Abundant life from the source of life to you,

Unconditional love from the God of love to you,

Let the blessings of God be always with you.

Amen.

Powerful and gentle God, bless Pauline,

And through your constant care let her

Understand that, though she may be

Little in the eyes of the world,

In your sight she is infinitely important.

Now and always be with her

Even to the end of time.

Penny (f) is short for Penelope, which in turn is derived from the Greek meaning 'thread.'

Penitent – may you know God's mercy,

Exhausted – may he give you rest,

Needing guidance – may he lead you,

Needing peace – may he bless you,

Yearning for love – may he hold you in his arms.

———————

Peter (m) means 'rock'. This was the nickname Jesus gave to his disciple, Simon, saying 'You are Peter [Rock] and on this rock I will build my Church' (Matthew 16.18, RSV). While with Jesus, Peter often acted rashly (trying and failing to walk on water) and failed (denying Jesus three times). But after Jesus' death Peter fulfilled the potential Jesus had seen in him and became the leader of the early Church.

Praise be to Jesus and his blessing be upon you.

Even as he called his friend Peter

To be the rock on which he built his Church,

Even so may he befriend you and build you,

Rock in your own right, on Peter's foundation.

Phillip (m) and Philippa (f) mean 'lover of horses', from two Greek words: *philein* (to love) and *hippos* (horse). Philip was one of Jesus' twelve disciples (John 1.43–45). For Philip (m) and Phillipa (f) see appendix.

Pour your love into Phillip's heart,

Heavenly Father, God of love;

Invincible love, stronger than death,

Love which hopes and bears all things,

Love which never comes to an end.

In your constant love bless him,

Protect him and keep him forever.

Pour your love into Philippa's heart,

Heavenly Father, God of love;

Invincible love, stronger than death,

Love which hopes and bears all things,

Infinite love which never ends.

Place your hands of blessing upon her,

Protect her and keep her

Always in your great love for her.

Phoebe (f) comes from the Greek meaning 'bright, shining, radiant and pure'. Paul commends 'our sister Phoebe, a deaconess' (Romans 16.1).

Purity of heart, shine within you

Hopefulness of spirit, shine before you

Openness of mind, shine around you

Eagerness for good, shine forth from you

Brightness of the eternal light, shine upon you

Evermore bless you and shine upon you

Phyllis (f) derives from the Greek for 'green bough'. The Bible makes many references to God's hands as a symbol of his action upon earth: e.g. Psalms 63.8, 98.1, 139.10.

Place hands of blessing on Phyllis, Lord;

Hold her in your loving embrace.

Your hand be ever in hers;

Lord, be her constant companion.

Lead her, guard her, keep her

In the way that will bring her

Safely and surely homeward with you.

Poppy (f) is named after the flower.

Pour your blessings of peace and grace

On your child Poppy, heavenly Father;

Prosper her passage through the uncharted future;

Protect her from peril and pestilence all the

Years of her life. Amen.

Quentin (m) comes from the Latin for 'fifth'; the name would originally have been given to a fifth son or child.

Quick to rescue, God protect you,

Understanding and patient, God forgive you,

Excelling all loves, God's love embrace you,

Night and day, God watch over you,

Trustworthy and true, God guide you,

Incomprehensible mystery, God reveal himself to you,

Now and always, God bless you.

RACHEL – *meaning ewe, suggesting gentleness and innocence.*

Rachel (f) or Rachael (f) is a Hebrew name meaning 'ewe' and
by association suggesting gentleness and innocence. In the Bible,
Rachel became Jacob's wife. Her father required Jacob to work
for him for seven years before they could marry, and for Jacob
the seven years 'seemed but a few days to him because of the love
he had for her' (Genesis 29.20, RSV). For Rachael see appendix.

Respond with compassion to Rachel, Lord,

Answer with love her calling to you,

Come alongside her when she is lonely,

Hold her when she is sad.

Everywhere she goes and everything she does,

Let your blessing be always upon her.

Ralph (m) derives from the old Norse words for 'counsel' and
'wolf' which in combination may mean 'wise and strong'.

Receive our thanks

And accept our prayers,

Loving Lord, for Ralph;

Protect him, bless him, and keep him

Happy and healthy, wise and strong.

Raymond (m) comes via the French from an Old German name combining the words for 'counsel' and 'protection'.

Righteous God, bless Raymond,

And grant him your protection in danger,

Your counsel in every dilemma.

May you keep him

Outwardly in safety, inwardly in grace,

Nightly in your peace,

Daily in your love.

Rebecca (f) is from the Hebrew, Rebekah, possibly meaning a 'heifer'. Rebekah was married to Isaac (Genesis 24.62–67) and was the mother of Esau and Jacob.

Risen Lord, the source of

Everything that gives new life;

Bless Rebecca with your grace,

Encourage her with your hope,

Comfort her with your peace,

Cherish her with your love,

And keep her in your care.

Reece (m) is an Anglicised version of the Welsh name, Rhys.

Risen Jesus, as you entered our world

Enter Reece's life and fill it with your blessings,

Enter his mind and fill it with your truth,

Come into his heart and fill it with your love,

Enter his spirit and fill it with your peace.

Reuben (m) comes from the Hebrew meaning, 'Behold, a son'.
In the Bible Reuben was the eldest son of Jacob (Genesis 29.32).

Regard Reuben, heavenly Father, as your son,

Eye him with your favour,

Upon his sleeping watch with peace,

Behold his rising with your blessings,

Espy the goodness within him,

Now and always look on him with love.

Rhiannon (f) comes from the Welsh meaning 'great queen' or 'goddess'.

Resurrection life, rise within you,

Heart of love, beat in your heart;

In God's blessing may you find peace,

And in his protection may

No evil overcome you

No trouble overwhelm you;

On you may God's light always shine,

Now and forever. Amen.

Rhys (m) is a Welsh name meaning 'ardent'.

Risen Jesus, bless Rhys:

His ardour give you joy;

Your love give him peace,

Strength and life.

Richard (m) means 'strong ruler'. This prayer plays on the similarity of sound between Richard and richer. For Ricky (m) see appendix.

Richer may you be through the gifts of God,

In service more willing by his grace,

Clearer in your vision through the wisdom of God,

Happier may you be in his blessings.

And may the love of God fulfil you more truly,

Raise you higher in his joy,

Draw you deeper into his peace.

Riley (m) is based on an old English place name meaning 'rye meadow'.

Ripe be your harvest,

Imperishable the gifts of God to you;

Long be your years,

Everlasting the love of God for you,

Your fruit be his blessing, his blessing your life.

Robert (m) comes from the German and means 'bright and famous'.

Refuge in the storm, shelter you

Oasis in the desert, refresh you

Beam in the darkness, guide you

Enemy of evil, defend you

Rock and foundation, support you

The God of all goodness, bless you.

Robin (m) is a diminutive of Robert.

Round you the arm of God to support you,

Over you the eye of God to watch for you,

Before you the light of God to guide you,

In you the love of God to bless you,

Next to you the Son of God beside you.

Roger (m) comes originally from the German meaning 'famous with the spear' or 'famous warrior'.

Round the seasons of life, God bless you:

On the soil of your soul may he sow his grace,

Growing seedlings of his love,

Encouraging them to maturity,

Reaping a rich harvest of joy.

Rory (m) derives from the Gaelic for 'red' (or red-haired) and 'king', which in combination suggest the meaning 'great king'.

Ruler of the universe, give Rory your blessings

Of guidance, protection and peace;

Reign in his heart with your mercy,

Your pity, your hope and your love.

Rose (f) is named after the flower. For Rosie (f) see appendix.

Rain softly, nurturing Lord,

On the soil of Rose's nature;

Shine warmly to open into flower

Every bud that grows from her soul.

Rosemary (f) is a plant name and means 'sea dew'. This prayer is based on the seven sayings of Jesus beginning "I am", all in John's gospel. These sayings go to the heart of who Jesus is and what he means to us (John 6:35; 8:12; 10:7; 10:11; 11:25; 14:6; 15:1).

Raise up Rosemary, Resurrection and Life,

Open your Way for her, you who are the Door,

Sustain her with your food, Bread of Life,

Enlighten her whole being, Light of the World.

May she know you more deeply, you who are Truth,

And abide in you, True Vine, that she may bear your fruit.

Rescue her, Good Shepherd, and gather her to you,

You, Lord Jesus, who are all good blessings to us.

Rowan (f) may come from the Irish Gaelic meaning 'red-haired' or from the rowan tree (mountain ash) with its red berries.

Round you, the arms of God to hold you

Over you, the hands of God to bless you

Within you, the Spirit of God to possess you

Ahead of you, the Son of God to lead you

Near you, the love of God to enfold you.

Rowena (f) derives from the Old English meaning 'fame' and 'joy'.

Round you, God protect you

Over you, God shine upon you

Within you, God inspire you

Embracing you, God love you

Near you, God remain beside you

And always God bless you.

Roy (m) comes either from Rory or from the French *roi* meaning 'king'.

Royal servant and humble king, reign

Over Roy with your justice, serve him with

Your love, govern him with your peace.

The name Ruby (f) comes from the red coloured precious stone (which is said to be associated with contentment and peace).

Riches from heaven bestow

Upon Ruby, Lord God;

Bless her with your priceless jewels;

Your joy, your peace, your love.

Ruth (f) comes originally from the Hebrew meaning possibly 'companion' or 'beauty'. In the Bible the book of Ruth tells the story of a Moabite woman who, having married a Jew and then been widowed, remained faithful to the God of Israel. Through her second marriage to Boaz she became great-grandmother to King David and appears in the genealogy of Jesus (Matthew 1.5).

Round you the peace and protection of God,

Under you his strength and support,

The love of God within your heart,

His blessings be ever upon you.

Ryan (m) may come from the Gaelic *ri* meaning 'king'.

Render to Ryan, heavenly King,

Your blessings of grace and your gracious promises

Always to stay with him, to guide and to guard,

Never to forsake him, in trouble or in need.

Sabine (f) comes from the name of the Italian Sabine tribe, which was subsumed by Rome.

Strong be God's defence around you,

And deep his peace inside you,

Bright his light to shine before you,

Infinite his love to keep you,

Numerous the blessings he showers upon you,

Eternal his life within you.

The name Sally (f) began as a shortened form of Sarah.

Source of all life,

All love and all joy,

Let your blessing be always upon Sally,

Look upon her with your favour,

Your protection and your grace.

Samantha (f) is derived from Samuel, possibly in combination with Anthea. This prayer was inspired by the hymn 'As the bridegroom to his chosen', a paraphrase of John Tauler by Emma Frances Bevan.

Source of all good things, be to Samantha

As the fruit is to the tree,

Manna to the hungry,

As the rain is to the desert,

North to the compass,

The lighthouse to the pilot,

Harbour to the sailor,

And the bridegroom to his beloved.

———

Samuel (m) is a Hebrew name meaning possibly 'he has listened' or 'asked of God'. Samuel was one of the judges and a major figure in the Old Testament, with two books (1 Samuel & 2 Samuel) named after him.

Source of all good things, be to Samuel

As the air is to the bird,

Manna to the hungry,

Umbilical cord to the child in the womb,

Earth to the seed,

Light to those who walk in darkness.

Sam (m/f) may be short for Samuel or Samantha (in which case change pronouns).

Should Sam forget you sometimes,
    remember him always, Lord;

Although he may stray somewhere from you,
    stay everywhere with him, Lord;

May your constant blessings keep him
    in your steadfast love.

Sandra (f) is a shortened form of Alexandra. For Sandy (f/m) see appendix.

Second by second, may God bless you,

And hour by hour, may God uphold you,

Night by night, may God rest you,

Day by day, may God renew you,

Restore you and refresh you,

And year after year may God love you.

Sara (f) and Sarah (f) come from the Hebrew meaning 'princess'.
In the Bible Sarah was the wife of Abraham (Genesis 17.15).

Sovereign Lord, love Sara as your daughter,

And crown her a princess in your kingdom.

Reign in her heart with mercy and peace,

And grant her your blessings forever.

Surround Sarah with your love, Lord,

Accompany her on the journey of life,

Reach out your hand to her when she needs help,

And bring her safely to end of her travelling,

Happy, fulfilled and blessed.

The name Sasha (f/m) comes from Russia and derives from
Alexander, meaning 'defender'.

Spirit of God bless you,

And keep you forever in his love.

Spirit of God defend you,

Help you, heal you, hold you,

And keep you in perfect peace.

Savannah (f) means a plain or grassland. For Savanna (f) see appendix.

Send your blessings like sunshine, Lord,

And like rain upon the ground of Savannah's soul;

Vast be the horizons open before her,

And wider still your love to encompass her;

Numerous the flowers and fruits she bears,

Numberless the gifts you sow in her,

And may all that grows upon her plain

Have roots deep in the soil of your peace.

Scarlett (f) is named after the bright and vibrant colour.

Sunshine of the soul, shine on you, Scarlett,

Creator of rainbows, colour your life brightly,

Artist of beauty, fill you with grace,

Rain from heaven, refresh your spirit,

Lyricist of life, write words for your song,

Essence of life, give you joy in your heart,

The God of peace fill your spirit with peace,

The God of love bless you now and always.

Scott (m) comes from a surname meaning 'Scottish'.

Spirit-waker, bless the life within you,

Cross-taker, share the burden of your pain,

Ocean-maker, still the waves beneath you,

Truth-speaker, give you wisdom and integrity,

Tyranny-breaker, deliver you from all evil.

Sean (m) is the Irish version of John.

Sunrise to sunset, God bless you and guide you;

Evening to morning, God bless you and rest you;

All times and all places, God bless you and guard you;

Now and forever, God bless you and love you.

Sebastian (m) comes either from the Latin (meaning 'of the town of Sebastos') or from the Greek (meaning 'respected'). Sebastian was a third century Roman martyr who, according to legend, was sentenced by the emperor Diocletian to be shot by arrows for his faith.

Strength of God support you,

Eternal light shine upon you,

Bread of life feed you,

Arms of God embrace you,

Shield of God defend you,

The whole armour of God protect you

In body, mind and spirit,

And the blessing of God be upon you,

Now and forever. Amen.

Selina (f) comes either from the Greek, meaning 'moon', or from the Latin meaning 'heavenly'.

Strong God, protect Selina,

Eternal God, be with her always,

Loving God, fill her heart with compassion,

Inspirational God, fill her soul with your hope,

Nurturing God, may she grow in your goodness,

All the days of her life.

Sharon (f) is a Biblical place name (Song of Solomon 2.1, Isaiah 65.10). The root of the word means 'song' or 'singer'.

Song of life, sing within Sharon,

Harmony of heaven, bring her peace,

Accompany her melody,

Retune her spirit to yours.

O God and composer of all,

Now and always bless her.

Sheila (f) is derived from Celia (meaning 'heavenly') via Sile, the Irish version of the name.

Son of God, be born again in you,

He who hung on the cross, bear your pain,

Easter Christ, renew your life,

Immortal love, bless you and keep you,

Light of the world, shine upon you,

Ascended Lord, raise you heavenwards.

Shirley (f) is an English place name meaning 'bright meadow'. Shirley was originally a boy's name but became a girl's name following Charlotte Bronte's novel, *Shirley* (1849).

Sure be God's defence around you,

High be his esteem for you,

Infinite be his love for you,

Radiant be his brightness upon you,

Long be his years for you,

Eternal be his life within you,

Yours be God's blessings for ever.

Siân (f) is a Welsh form of Jane.

Sunrise to sunset, God bless you and keep you;

In your learning and working, God bless you and guide you;

Âsleep and at leisure, God bless you and rest you;

Now and forever, God bless you and love you.

The name Sienna (f) refers to the Italian city, which also gives its name to a clay used to make some of the earliest pigments in painting, the reddish brown raw sienna and burnt sienna. For Siena (f) omit either the third or fourth line.

Subtle the shades of God's peace within you,

Intense the hues of God's joy,

Extensive the spectrum of God's blessings upon you,

New and original the palate of his gifts to you,

Never-fading the pigment of his love for you,

And bright the shining of his light.

Simon (m) comes from the Hebrew Simeon meaning 'he who hears'. There are two Simons among the twelve disciples: Simon Peter and Simon called the Canaanite or Zealot (Matthew 10.2–4). For Simone (f) see appendix.

Speak, Lord, to your servant Simon,

In intimations of guidance and glory;

May he hear your still, small voice

Over the earthquake, wind and fire,

Narrating your blessings upon him.

In the Old Testament Simeon (f) was one of Jacob's twelve sons. In the New Testament Simeon was a devout man who recognised that the baby Jesus would be a light to lighten the nations and the glory of God's people (Luke 2.32).

Speak, Lord, to your servant Simeon,

In intimations of guidance and glory;

May he hear your still, small voice

Even through the earthquake, wind and fire,

Over the storms of passion and the murmurs of self-will,

Narrating your love and your blessings upon him.

Sinead (f) is an Irish form of Janet. The first and last words of this prayer echo the sound of the two syllables in Sinead's name.

Shining on you, may the Eternal Light,

Illuminate your way;

Nourishing you, may the Bread of Life,

Enrich your hungry soul;

And may the God of love bless you,

Defend you and come to your aid.

Skye (f) comes either from the vocabulary word 'sky' (which in turn derives from the Norse for 'cloud') or from the Isle of Skye in Scotland.

Shower your blessings on Skye like raindrops,

Keep her, Lord, in the sunshine of your love,

Your Spirit blow freshly upon her each day,

Each sunset bring with it your rest and peace.

Sophie (f) means 'wisdom' in Greek. In the book of Proverbs Wisdom is personified as a woman (Proverbs 1.20, 9.1). For Sofia (f) and Sophia (f) see appendix.

Shepherd God, guide Sophie,

Omniscient God, grant her wisdom,

Protector God, keep her safe,

Healing God, give her wholeness and health,

Inspirational God, be the creativity within her,

Eternal God, fill her with your love.

Stanley (m) comes from a place name meaning 'stone field or clearing'. There is a reference in the third and fourth lines to Romans 8.39.

So may God protect you

That with him you need fear nothing,

And so may God love you that

Nothing can ever separate you.

Let the blessing of God be

Evermore upon you,

Your family and all you love.

Stella (f) means 'star' (from Latin). Its use as a name began as a title for the Virgin Mary, *Stella Maris* meaning 'star of the sea'.

Shine upon Stella, Jesus, Light of the World,

To protect her, encourage her,

Enlighten and nurture her.

Let your love warm her like the morning sun,

Let your peace guide her like the stars by night,

And let your blessings shine ever upon her.

Stephen (m) means 'garland' or 'crown' (from the Greek *stephanos*). Stephen was the first deacon of the early Church (Acts 6.5) and the first Christian martyr, stoned to death while he prayed to God to forgive his persecutors (Acts 7.54–8.1). For Stefan (m), Steve (m/f) and Stephanie (f) see appendix.

Set a garland of grace on Stephen's head;

Tailor a garment of blessings for him,

Embroidered with joy on a fabric of peace;

Place it round his shoulders, Lord,

His cloak of defence against all evil,

Every stitch sewn by your very own hand,

Neat with your care and strong with your love.

Set a garland of grace on Steven, Lord;

Tailor a wardrobe of blessings for him,

Each garment bespoke and unique,

Vestments fashioned from the fabric of peace,

Every stitch sewn by your hand, O Lord,

Neat with your care and strong with your love.

Stewart (m) comes from a Scottish surname meaning 'steward' and Stuart (m) derives from a French version of Stewart.

Strength of God, sustain you,

Tenderness of God, embrace you,

Energy of God, quicken you,

Wisdom of God, guide you,

Abundance of God, provide for you,

Riches of God, equip you,

The blessing of God be always with you.

Strength of God, sustain you,

Truth of God, guide you,

Understanding of God, enlighten you;

Ardour of God, enthuse you,

Riches of God, equip you,

The blessing of God be always with you.

Summer (f) is named after the season of the year.

Shine like the sun at the height of the year

Upon Summer, O God and sun of our soul;

May she flourish in the warmth of your love,

May her hours be bright in the light of your life,

Evening be balmy, her twilight be long,

Resting in the blessing of your peace.

Susan (f) and Suzanne (f) derive from the Biblical name,
Susanna (Luke 8.3) which comes from the Hebrew for 'lily'. For
Sue (f) see appendix.

Since before your life began

Until the end of time,

So long may God's love for you be;

And so may his blessings be upon you

Now and always.

Spirit of God, grant to you:

Understanding and compassion,

Zeal for justice and peace,

Appreciation of all that is good,

Never-ending, unconditional love,

New blessings today, tomorrow,

Evermore and evermore.

Sydney (f/m) comes either via the French from St. Denis, or more probably from the old English, meaning 'wide river island'.

Surround Sydney like a river round an island,

Your waters, Lord, lapping upon her shores;

Downstream may she find the depths of your mercy,

New life upstream, welling up from your source;

Every day may your blessings flow upon her,

Your powerful current of love and peace.

Sylvia (f) comes from the Latin meaning 'woods' or 'forest'.

Send your blessings on Sylvia, Lord,

Your peace on all her ways.

Let your Spirit

Visit and dwell

In her soul forever

And your love reside in her heart.

Taylor (f/m) comes from a surname, indicating the work of a tailor. Originally a boy's name, it is now more frequently used for a girl.

The God of peace tailor

A garment of blessings for you;

Your perfect fit, your unique style.

Let it be a cloak of God's warmth,

Of his comfort and protection,

Richly woven with his love.

Teresa (f) comes from the Greek meaning either 'reaping and harvest' or 'guarding and watching'. The name has been borne by three notable saintly women: St. Teresa of Avila (1515–1582), St. Thérèse de Lisieux (1873–1897) and Mother Teresa of Calcutta (1910–1997).

The Lord God guard you,

Evermore watch over you,

Raise you up from every fall,

Evermore hold you in his love,

Sow his blessings within your soul,

And reap a harvest of peace and joy.

Terry (m) may be a shortened form of Terence, or may derive from a word of Germanic origin meaning 'power'.

The strength of God be your support,

Energy of God your power;

Resources of God your replenishment,

Refuge of God your defence,

Your life be filled with God's blessings.

Theo (m) comes from the Greek *theos* meaning 'God'. It was originally a shortened version of either Theodore ('God's gift') or Theobald ('brave for the people') or Theophilus ('God lover'). In the Bible both the gospel of Luke and the book of Acts are addressed to Theophilus (Luke 1.3 & Acts 1.1).

The God of love be in your

Heart and your caring, your head and your thinking,

Eyes and your looking, mouth and your speaking,

On your coming in and going out, God's blessing.

Thomas (m) was one of Jesus' twelve disciples, nicknamed 'doubting Thomas' because he said he would not believe in Jesus' resurrection until he could see and touch Jesus' wounds. Despite his initial scepticism, Thomas was the first disciple to acknowledge Jesus as his Lord and God (John 20.28). Thomas comes from the Aramaic for 'twin'.

The God of love bless you,

Hold you, and help you to

Overcome life's obstacles,

Marvel at life's mysteries,

Assist those in adversity,

Share of your gifts unselfishly.

Through difficulty, danger, maze and marsh,

Over unmapped mountains and troubled waters,

May God lead you, carry you and bless you.

Tia (f) has many possible origins in different languages: 'auntie' in Spanish, 'princess' in Greek, 'daylight' or 'deity' in Indo-European languages, or 'joy' from the Latin. This prayer refers to Psalm 126.5–6.

Though you sow in tears, may you reap in songs of joy,

If you reap in joy, may God bless your harvest,

And may your harvest be rich in peace and love.

Tilly (f) is a shortened form of Matilda.

Till evil is banished, may God keep you

In his peace and protection,

Let God guide you, till you reach your journey's end,

Let God bless you, till the end of time itself,

Yet even then may God keep you in his love.

Timothy (m) means 'honouring God' or 'honoured by God'.
Timothy was a friend and companion of St. Paul (Acts 16.1–3).
Two letters of St. Paul are addressed to Timothy.

The God of peace protect you

In your times of danger and difficulty.

May the peace of God be within you

On your days of fear and anxiety.

Then may he, whom you honour in worship,

Honour you with blessings and ever remain

Your peace, your protection, your God.

Toby (m) comes from the Hebrew name Tobias meaning 'the
Lord is good'. The story of Tobias is to be found in the book of
Tobit in the apocrypha.

To God who gave you life, be thanks and praise,

On God who guards you, may you place your trust,

By God who loves you, may you be deeply blessed,

Yesterday, today, tomorrow and always.

TREVOR – *a place name meaning great homestead.*

Tracy (f) probably relates to the place name of Thrace. For Tracey (f) see appendix.

Traces of glory brighten your vision,

Rumours of God whisper in your ear,

Aromas of God perfume your thinking.

Colours of heaven be the weft to your warp,

Your fabric of life be shot through with blessings.

Trevor (m) comes from the Welsh and is a place name meaning 'great homestead'.

Truly may God guide you,

Radiantly may God shine upon you,

Evermore may God love you,

Vibrantly may God live within you,

Outwardly and inwardly may God keep you,

Richly may God bless you.

Trinity (f) derives from the Latin for 'three' and refers to the Holy Trinity; the Father, Son and Holy Spirit (Matthew 28.19).

The God of creation give you fullness of life,

Redeeming Son, keep you safe in his care,

Indwelling Spirit, abide in you always.

Now may the threefold blessing of God be

In your heart and your mind and your spirit,

To fill you with love and peace and joy,

Yesterday, today and forever.

The name Tyler (m) comes originally from the occupation of making tiles or tiling roofs.

The house of your life be founded on God,

Your walls be God's defence;

Let your house be warmed by the love of God,

Every room filled with God's peace,

Roofed and tiled by God's blessings.

Una (f) may come from the Irish for 'lamb' or the Latin for 'one'. The first line of this prayer refers to Deuteronomy 33.27.

Underneath you, God's everlasting arms to raise you,

Near you, God's strong arms to defend you,

Around you, God's loving arms to embrace you.

Ursula (f) comes from the Latin for 'she-bear'.

Until all darkness ends, Lord,

Radiate your light on Ursula;

Send your blessings upon her.

Until all conflicts cease, Lord,

Let your peace and love

Abide in her heart forever.

VALERIE – *Vine of God.*

Valerie (f) means 'healthy' or 'strong'. This prayer draws on the image of Jesus as the true vine (John 15.1–8). For Valeria add 'And' at the beginning of the last line.

Vine of God

Abide in you;

Let your branches

Ever abide in God;

Rich be your harvest

In the love of God;

Eternal be God's blessings upon you.

———

The name Vanessa (f) was invented by Jonathan Swift and is based on the name of a young woman he loved called Esther Vanhomrigh.

Vain be the powers of evil

Against God's shield around you;

Never may the light of God fail

Even though darkness surround you.

Strong be the love of God for you,

Strong be the peace of God within you,

And strong be the blessings of God upon you.

Vera (f) comes from the Latin meaning 'truth' or 'faith'.

Very great be God's faith in you

Eternal, God's truth in you,

Rich be God's blessings upon you

Abundant, God's life within you.

Veronica (f) comes from the Latin meaning 'true image'.
According to legend Jesus met St. Veronica as he carried his cross.
She offered him a cloth to wipe his face and the cloth retained
the image of his features.

Vaster than oceans, God's grace to you,

Even deeper than space, God's peace,

Rarer than jewels, God's gifts to you,

Older than the world, God's wisdom,

Newer than today, God's life within you,

Intimate as thought, God's closeness,

Countless as the stars, God's blessings upon you,

And greatest of all, God's love.

Victoria (f) means 'victory'. Many early Christians were called Victorius, after Christ's victory over sin and death (1 Corinthians 15.55–56).

Victorious God, defend you,

Invincible God, shield you,

Conquering Christ, save you,

Triumphant Christ, raise you.

Omnipotent Spirit, empower you,

Reigning Spirit, lead you,

Immortal love, fill you,

Almighty Trinity, bless you.

Victorious God, defend Vicky,

Invincible God, shield her,

Conquering Christ, save her,

King of all Kings, govern her,

Your blessing be always upon her.

Virginia (f) comes from the Roman family name Verginius, which in turn was derived from the Latin *virgo* meaning 'maiden'.

Very God of very God,

Incarnate Word,

Risen Lord,

Grant to Virginia

Infinite peace,

Never-ending love,

Inextinguishable light,

And eternal life.

Wayne (m) comes from the surname meaning 'a carter'.

With your light to guide him,

And your presence beside him,

Your love inside him,

Now may your blessing, Eternal God,

Evermore rest upon Wayne.

The name Wendy (f) was invented by J. M. Barrie for a character in Peter Pan. Apparently the idea came from a little girl who could not pronounce the word 'friend' so she called him 'my fwendy'.

When she is joyful, Lord, rejoice with Wendy,

Embrace and comfort her when she weeps,

Never leave her when she needs a friend,

Defend her when in danger and grant her

Your blessing when she calls upon your name.

William (m) comes from the German 'Wilhelm' (*wil* meaning 'will' & *helm* meaning 'protection'). Billy (m/f) may be short for William or Wilhelmina. For Billie (f/m) see appendix.

Wherever you go, whatever you do,

In all your journey through life,

Let the will of God guide you;

Let the protection of God surround you

In every danger and difficulty;

And in all your learning and your working

May God bless you with joy and fulfilment.

Blessings of the love of God be

In your heart forever;

Let his peace be ever in your spirit;

Let the grace of Christ fill everything

You think or speak or do.

Willow (f) is named after the tree which often grows by water (see Psalm 1.3).

Where your roots grow may there always be water,

In ground firm and fertile may your roots take hold,

Let winds bend your boughs but never break them,

Let there be sun and warmth but never a drought,

On you may God's light always shine,

With blessings of love and joy and peace.

Xander (m) is a shortened form of Alexander.

e**X**tend your watch of love over Xander,

And multiply your blessings upon him, Lord;

Never diminish your peace within him,

Deepen in him your well of life,

Ever increase your love for him,

Remain with him for evermore.

Xavier (m) derives from the Arabic meaning 'bright'. St. Francis Xavier (1506–1552) was a Jesuit missionary in India and the Far East.

e**X**celling all loves, God's love for you,

Abiding for ever, God's love for you,

Vanquishing death, God's love for you,

Infinitely deep, God's love for you,

Enduring all things, God's love for you,

Richer than all things, God's love for you.

YVONNE – *from the French meaning yew.*

Yvonne (f) comes from the old French meaning 'yew'.

Your blessing, Lord, be upon Yvonne,

Vouchsafe to her your peace,

Open to her the door to new life,

Navigate her way through dangerous waters,

Nurse her to health through every hurt,

Embrace her forever in your love.

Zachary (m) comes from Zachariah or Zechariah which means, in Hebrew, 'Jehovah has remembered'. Zechariah (Zacharias in the New Testament Greek) was the father of John the Baptist (Luke 1). This prayer contains references to Luke 1.8,13, and Luke 1.78–79, from Zechariah's prophecy known as the Benedictus. For Zac (m) and Zak (m) see appendix.

Zealously may you seek God;

Abundantly may he bless you.

Constantly may he hear your prayer;

Humbly may you serve him.

And may the dawn from on high

Radiate light upon you to guide

Your steps into the way of peace.

Zara (f) is from the Arabic meaning 'flower' or 'splendour'.

Zeal for the good in her longing;

Appreciation of others in her loving;

Respect for the earth in her living:

All these grant to Zara, Lord God.

Zoe (f) is Greek for 'life' and is the root of our word zoology. There are two Greek words for life: *zoe* and *bios* (the root of our word biology). In the New Testament *zoe* is used more specifically to mean spiritual life as opposed to physical life (*bios*). So when Jesus says, 'I am the bread of life' or 'the resurrection and the life' or talks of 'the spring of water welling up to eternal life' the word *zoe* is always used. The phrase 'oil of gladness' comes from Isaiah 61.3.

Zest of true life, may God flavour your living;

Oil of gladness, may God anoint your loving;

Essence of love, may God suffuse your being.

APPENDIX

Abba, Father, bless you:

Bless you with joy in your sadness,

Bless you with light in your darkness,

In your need, bless you with plenty,

Every day God bless you with his love.

Abba, Father, bless you:

Bless you with joy in your sadness;

Bless you with light in your darkness;

Your whole life be blessed with his love.

As the air you breathe, God fill you and inspire you,

In the water of life, God refresh you and cleanse you,

Dependable as the earth, God support you on your journey,

Enkindled as fire, God warm you and protect you,

Now may God bless you and always be with you.

As the armour to the soldier,

Like a lighthouse to the sailor,

As the parachute to the pilot,

So may God's love

Defend and deliver you.

As the lifeboat to the lost

In the stormy sea, so may God

Rescue and restore you.

As the armour to the soldier,

Like a lighthouse to the sailor,

In darkness and danger,

So may God be to you

To defend and deliver you.

As the lifeboat to the lost,

In the stormy sea, so may God

Rescue and restore you.

As God turned his Son's death to new life,

Let him turn your sorrows to joys,

Endings to beginnings,

eXchange your troubles for peace,

And your burdens for blessings.

As you turned your Son's death to new life,

Lord, turn Alexandra's troubles to blessings,

Endings to beginnings,

eXchange her sorrows for joys.

And as you promised

Never to forsake those who love you,

Defend her against every danger,

Remain with her and bless her for ever.

Amen.

As you turned your Son's death to new life,

Lord, turn Alexis's sorrows to joys,

Endings to beginnings,

eXchange her troubles for your peace;

In these and many unexpected ways

Surprise her with your blessings.

Adorn Alicia,

Lord of all loveliness,

In robes of peace and love and joy;

Clothe her in strength and dignity,

In the garment of salvation,

And crown her with your blessings.

Adorn Alisha,

Lord of all loveliness,

In robes of righteousness and holiness;

Strength and dignity be her clothing,

Her cloak be your peace and protection,

And your love be a crown upon her head.

As night follows day,

Let the peace of God be upon your resting;

Let the blessing of God be upon your rising,

As day follows night,

Now and evermore.

Almighty God,

Lord of all loveliness,

Let Allison be adorned

In robes of righteousness and holiness;

Strength and dignity be her clothing;

On her shoulders place the garment of salvation,

None other than Jesus Christ himself.

All the days of your life,

May God bless you,

Encourage and equip you,

Lead and enlighten you,

Instruct and inspire you,

Embrace and love you.

Around and within, the protection of God for you,

Now and forever, the blessing of God for you,

Deep and wide, the love of God for you,

Restful and refreshing, the peace of God for you,

Everywhere and always, the guidance of God for you,

Abundant and vibrant, the life of God for you.

As some have ministered to strangers,

Not knowing they were angels,

God send his angels to you.

Entertain them, serve them;

Let them minister to you and bless you.

As some have ministered to strangers,

Not knowing they were angels,

God send his angels to you.

Entertain them, serve them;

Let them also minister to your needs,

Inspire you with good news,

Nurse you and heal you,

And through them may God bless you.

According to God's promises, and by his grace,

Neither death, nor life, nor things present, nor things to come –

Nothing in all creation – can separate you from his love:

Even so may God keep you in his love for ever.

According to God's promises, and by his grace,

Neither death, nor life, nor things present, nor things to come –

Nothing in all creation can separate you from his love:

Even so may God keep you safe in his love,

The love of God dwell in your heart and mind,

The God of love bless you and keep you,

Evermore and evermore.

A blessing of life to you, first of all,

Next, of growth, in body and spirit,

Then of peace, which this world cannot give,

Over all, a blessing of love to you –

Never-ending, ever-hoping, all-enduring love.

A blessing of life to you, first of all –

New life, life in all its fullness;

Then a blessing of love to you,

Overflowing from the heart of God to you –

Never-ending, ever-hoping, all-enduring love,

In the name of the father who loves you as his child,

And of the son who gave his life for you.

A blessing of life to you, first of all –

New life, life in all its fullness;

Then a blessing of love to you,

Overflowing from the heart of God to you –

Never-ending, ever-hoping, all-enduring love,

In the name of the loving father,

Of the risen son, and of the living Spirit.

A blessing of life to you, first of all,

Next, of growth, in body and spirit,

Then of peace, which this world cannot give,

Over all, a blessing of love to you –

Never-ending, ever-hoping, all-enduring love,

Your heavenly father's love for you.

At each need a blessing from God:

Refreshment when you are weary,

In your hunger, God's feeding,

After sadness, his comfort,

New peace after trouble,

New hope after disappointment,

And after death, new life.

Bestow your love on Beverly, Lord,

Every moment of every day;

Vouchsafe to keep her in your peace

Every day of every year;

Raise her up from every fall;

Lord, every year of evermore,

Your blessing be upon her.

Blessings of the love of God be

In your heart forever;

Let his peace be ever in your spirit;

Let the grace of Christ be

In everything you think,

Everything you say or do.

Be your strength drawn from the power of God,

Refreshment from the water of life,

Inner calm from the peace of God;

All you seek be with God's guidance,

Nothing you do be without God's love,

Nowhere you go be without God's blessing,

Always and everywhere. Amen.

Be your strength drawn from the power of God,

Refreshment from the water of life,

Your inner calm from the peace of God;

All you do be within the love of God,

Nowhere you go be without God's blessing.

Bless Briony,

Risen Lord Jesus;

In her need provide for her,

On her journeys guide her,

Nurture her with your love,

Your peace and your joy.

Before you the blessing of God to guide you,

Round you the blessing of God to embrace you,

Over you the blessing of God to shelter you,

Near you the blessing of God to protect you,

Within you the blessing of God to be your peace,

Your joy, your life, your all,

Now and for ever. Amen.

Constantly may God guard you,

Ardently may God love you,

Richly may God bless you,

Loyally may God ever remain

Your friend, your saviour, your all.

Circle Carol with your blessings, Lord,

And dance with her in your joy;

Ring her round with your protection,

O Lord, surround her with your peace,

Let your love embrace her for ever.

Circle Carolyn with your blessings, Lord,

And dance with her in your joy;

Ring her round with your protection,

O Lord, surround her with your care.

Let her steps remain within

Your circumference of peace;

Now and always embrace her with love.

Christ Jesus, bless Charlie:

Help him when he feels

Anxious or afraid;

Reassure him when he is

Lost or lacking in confidence;

Inspire him through all his

Employment and enjoyment.

Christ Jesus be in your heart, as

He holds you forever in his,

Raising you up, when you are brought low,

In the power of his resurrection.

So may the Bread of Life feed you,

The Light of the World lead you

In the way, the truth and the life,

Now and always.

Amen and Amen.

Clear as the cloudless sky, God's peace to you,

Like the breeze off the ocean, God's life for you,

As bright as a mountain stream, God's joy to you,

In depth as the deepest sea, God's love to you,

Refreshing as pure spring water, God's spirit within you,

Even more than the myriad stars, God's blessings to you.

Clear as the cloudless sky, God's peace to you,

Like the breeze off the ocean, God's life for you,

As bright as a mountain stream, God's joy to you,

Refreshing as pure spring water, God's spirit within you,

As numerous as the stars above, God's blessings to you.

Christ guard and guide you

On every path which lies before you;

Let the blessing of God be upon you

Each moment of each day of your life.

Dear God, be with Daniella,

Above her to watch over her,

Near her to protect her,

In her to inspire and instruct her,

Embracing her with your love,

Leading her on her life-long journey.

Let your blessing be upon her

And remain with her forever.

Day by day, God grow within you,

Evening by evening, God refresh you,

Blessing after blessing God lavish upon you,

Round and round, God's love embrace you,

Arm in arm, God walk with you.

Embrace Elizabeth in your grace,

Loving and life-giving Lord.

Inspire and increase in her

Zest for life and zeal for good,

And bless her now and always.

Every moment of each day,

Let the peace of God give you strength,

In your heart may the love of God abide,

Over your ways may the God of love preside,

The Father, the Son and the Spirit bless you,

The blessings of God be ever upon you.

Every moment of each day,

Let the peace of God give you strength,

Let the strength of God protect you,

In your heart may the love of God abide,

Over your ways may the God of love preside,

The Father, the Son and the Spirit bless you,

The blessings of God be ever upon you.

Everywhere she sails on the sea of life, keep Evie's

Vessel safe in storm and strait;

In uncharted waters guide her

Even to her destination, her haven with you.

Everywhere she sails on the sea of life, guide Eva's

Vessel through fog and storm and strait,

And bring her safe to her harbour home.

First may the blessing of God be upon you

In your years of growing and learning to live,

Next through your working and learning to give

Let the blessing of God stay with you.

And finally in your years of maturity

Yours be the blessings of God for ever.

First may the blessing of God be upon you

In your years of growing and learning to live,

Next through your working and learning to give

Let the blessing of God stay with you.

Even to the final years of your life,

Yours be the blessings of God for ever.

Father, bless Frances and let her bring

Reconciliation where there is discord,

Affection where there is coldness of heart,

New hope where there is despair,

Comfort where there is sadness,

Encouragement where there is disappointment;

So may she be an instrument of your peace.

Glory be to God who gave you life,

And peace on earth to you whom he loves.

Blessings of God be in your spirit,

Righteousness of God in your heart,

In your understanding be God's wisdom,

Everything you do be in God's strength,

Let the grace of God be ever with you,

Let the love of God be ever within you,

Ever may God's glory shine upon you.

God of life, sow your blessings in the

Earth of Georgia's spirit.

Over time may they send down

Roots deep and sustaining,

Growing a harvest abundant

In love and joy and peace.

Amen.

God of life, sow your blessings in the

Earth of Georgina's spirit.

Over time may they send down

Roots deep and sustaining,

Growing a harvest abundant

In love and joy and peace,

Now and forever.

Amen.

God bless you with peace,

Embrace you with love,

Relieve your suffering,

And calm your fears.

Let God's blessing be with you,

Day and night:

In you to comfort you,

Near you to defend you,

Evermore upon you to keep you.

God bless you and dwell within you,

In your heart may his love make a home,

Let his peace abide in each room of your life,

Let his light shine out from the windows of your soul.

God grant you his generous gifts of grace,

Riches beyond price, yet freely given;

Abundant life, unconditional love,

Countless blessings, unbounded mercy,

Inexaustible hope, unfailing protection,

Enduring peace and joy without end.

God weep with you when you are weeping,

When you rejoice, rejoice with you;

Each new day may God bless your rising,   ‘

Night after night God bless your resting.

Holy God, hold Hailey in your love

And enfold her in your peace,

In your comfort, in your protection.

Let your blessing be on her daily;

Every night your blessing of rest,

Your blessing of new life every rising.

Holy God, hold Haley in your love

And enfold her in your peace;

Let your blessing be on her daily;

Every night your blessing of rest,

Your blessing of new life every rising.

Heavenly Father, bless Helena now and to eternity,

Eternal God, guide her with your light,

Light of the world, shine on her with Easter glory,

Easter Lord, give her new life in your name,

Name above all names, protect her with your might,

Almighty Father, bring her safely to heaven.

Heavenly Father, bless Helene now and to eternity,

Eternal God, guide her with your light,

Light of the world, shine on her with Easter glory,

Easter Lord, give her new life in your name,

Name above all names, protect her to the last,

Everlasting Father, bring her safely to heaven.

Home to our restless hearts, God draw you to his love;

Ear to our spirit's voice, God listen to your longings;

Nourishment to our deepest hungers, God feast you,

Refreshment to our souls, God give you fullness of life,

Illumination to our path, God shine before you,

Ease to our weariness, God fill you with his peace,

The Spirit of truth, guide you into all truth,

The Son of God, be always with you,

And the Father of all creation, bless you forever.

Holy God, pour the sunshine and rain

Of your life-giving blessings on Hollie;

Let her be rooted and grounded in your love;

Let the fruit she bears be bright as berries;

In every time and season may she be

Evergreen all the years of her life.

In your growing and your learning,

Spirit of God nurture you.

As you suffer and as you hurt

Be the healing of God within you.

Every journey that you make,

Let the blessing of God be with you.

In your growing and your learning,

Spirit of God nurture you.

As you suffer and as you hurt

Be the healing of God within you.

Every choice that you make,

Let the wisdom of God guide you.

Let the blessing of God go with you

All the journeys that you undertake.

Joy be yours, and comfort in sadness,

Affection be yours, and the company of friends,

Courage be yours, and protection in danger,

Kindness be yours, and concern for those in need,

Serenity be yours, and peace which the world cannot give,

Obedience be yours, to the will of our heavenly father,

New blessings be yours, and the love of God forever.

Jesus be your help in need

And walls of defence in danger.

Deeply may he love you,

Eternally may he bless you,

Never may he forsake you.

Jesus bless you with his life and peace,

And keep you in his light and love,

Now and here, everywhere and always.

Jesus bless you with his risen life,

And keep you in his love and peace;

Never-ending, unconditional love,

Everlasting, abundant life,

The peace which passes all understanding.

Jesus bless you with his life and light,

And keep you in his love and peace;

Newness of life,

Inextinguishable light,

Never-ending love,

Everlasting peace.

Jesus fill Jayne with your risen life,

And keep her in your love,

Your peace and your blessings;

Never-ending love, perfect peace,

Everlasting life, countless blessings.

Jesus be with you,

Evermore love you,

Never leave you,

Nor forsake you,

And forever bless you.

Jesus be with you,

Evermore love you,

Never leave you,

Nor forsake you,

In trouble care for you,

Every day bless you.

Jesus bless you,

Evermore love you,

Never leave you,

Nor ever cease to be

Your saviour and your friend.

Jesus, joy-giver, grant Jessie happiness,

Essence of life, bless her abundantly,

Source of strength, guard her,

Spring of love, refresh her soul,

Inspirer of truth, lead her in your way,

Everlasting light, shine upon her.

Jesus bless you and walk with you

On every path of your journey,

And grant that by his guidance and protection

No temptation may ever lead you from the way

Nor any trouble you encounter

Ever overcome you.

Jesus' peace be in your heart,

Understanding and justice be in your head,

Dancing and joy be in your spirit;

Your gifts from the God who loves you.

Joy from God's laughter be with you,

Understanding from God's word guide you,

Love from God's heart embrace you,

Inner peace from God's spirit fill you,

And blessings of God's grace be upon you

Now and always. Amen.

Joy from God's laughter be with you,

Understanding from God's word guide you,

Love from God's heart embrace you,

Inner peace from God's spirit fill you,

Energy from God's life abound in you.

Joy from God's laughter be with you,

Understanding from God's word guide you,

Love from God's heart embrace you,

Inner peace from God's spirit fill you,

Energy from God's life abound in you.

The blessings of God's grace be upon you.

King of heaven bless you,

And keep you in his loving care;

The Spirit of God grant you

Every talent and gift you need;

Let the Son of God be with you,

Your source of peace and joy,

Now and all your days.

King of peace bless you

And keep you in perfect peace;

The God of love bless you,

Hold you in his everlasting arms;

Abba, Father, bless you,

Remain with you always;

Inextinguishable Light bless you,

Now and always guide you,

Evermore shine upon you.

King of peace bless you

And keep you in perfect peace;

The God of love bless you,

Hold you in his everlasting arms;

Risen Lord bless you,

Your life be his and his be yours,

Now and for evermore.

Kindly Lord, bless Kaylee

And by your strength,

Your grace and your guidance,

Let her follow the difficult road,

Entering through the narrow gate –

Even the way that leads to life.

Key to life's mystery, open your blessings to Kieron,

Infinite love of life, embrace him with your blessings,

Energy of life, empower him with your blessings,

Radiant light of life, shine your blessings upon him,

Overflowing life, pour your blessings upon him,

Newness of life, bless him afresh each day.

King of peace, pour your peace

Into the cup of Kimberly's soul.

Maker and care-taker of all that is,

Bless her and keep her in your care.

Everlasting light, stronger than darkness,

Radiate upon her your life-giving light.

Love divine, stronger than death, grant her

Your love and life eternal.

Kindly Lord, grant Kyle
Your blessing and your guidance:
Let him find the way that leads to life,
Even though the road may be hard and the gate narrow.

Let God's blessings be
Above you to watch over you
Under you to support you
Round you to protect you
Encircling you to embrace you
Near you always to comfort you.

Let the love of God be
Above you to watch over you
Under you to support you
Round you to protect you
Encircling you to embrace you
Near you to comfort you.
Christ bless you and keep you
Everywhere and evermore.

Let the blessings of God be

Above you to watch over you

Under you to support you

Round you to protect you

In you to strengthen you

Encircling you to embrace you

Let the blessings of God be

Above you to watch over you

Within you to strengthen you

Round you to protect you

In front of you to lead you

Encircling you to embrace you

Let all your strength be drawn from God,

Every path you take be guided by God,

Over all your ways may God protect you,

Now and all your days may God bless you.

Let God turn your troubles to blessings,

Endings to beginnings,

eXchange your disappointment for hope,

In place of sorrow may he bring you joy.

Lord, grant Lillian your purity,

In all she thinks and says and does;

Let her be blessed with your love;

Let her remain in your peace,

In your protection,

And in your mercy,

Now and always.

Lord, grant Lilly your purity,

In all she thinks and says and does.

Let her be blessed with peace and love,

Let her remain always in your protection,

Your guidance and your care.

Look with your gracious favour, Lord,

Upon Luca and pour upon him

Countless blessings in your constant love,

All the days of his life.

Let your heart be filled with God's love,

Your spirit with his peace;

Night by night, God replenish your rest,

Day by day, your hope;

And the blessing of God be always with you.

Let your heart be filled with God's love,

Your spirit be filled with his peace;

Night by night, God replenish your rest,

Day by day, your hope;

Second by second, God keep you in his care,

And hour by hour, in his grace,

Year after year, in his blessings.

May the son of God bless you,

And give you your daily bread,

Deliver you from evil,

In times of temptation

Strengthen you to do his will

On earth, as it is in heaven,

Now and forever. Amen.

May God be to you a warm summer sun,

And the autumn harvest within you,

In wintry storms may he be your shelter,

And a springtime of hope and new life.

May the Lord be with you

And do great things for you;

In his graciousness may he bless you,

Regarding your lowliness with his favour.

Morning by morning God renew your hope

And evening by evening God restore your peace

Round you and within you God protect you

Constantly and unconditionally God love you

In time and for eternity God bless you

And here and in heaven God be with you.

May God bless you

And keep you in his love,

Refresh your soul,

Grant you his peace;

Embrace you when you are sad,

Reassure you and ever remain

Your maker and redeemer.

May the Lord be with you

And do great things for you,

Regarding your lowliness with his favour.

In his graciousness may he bless you

And fill you with his joy,

His peace and his love.

May the Lord be with you

And do great things for you,

Regarding your lowliness with his favour.

In his graciousness may he bless you

And fill you with his love,

Now and always.

May the Lord be with you

And do great things for you,

Regarding your lowliness with his favour.

In his grace,

And according to his word,

Neither death, nor life, nor things present, nor things to come –

Nothing in all creation – can separate you from his love:

Even so may God keep you in his love for ever.

May the Lord be with you

And do great things for you,

Regarding your lowliness with his favour.

In every way may you be blessed;

Every day may you know his love.

May the Lord be with you

And do great things for you,

Regarding your lowliness with his favour.

In the power of the Holy Spirit may he

Overshadow you and bring to birth

New life and love within you.

May the Lord be with you
And find favour with you,
Regarding your lowliness
Yet doing great things for you;
And in his graciousness
May God bless you and keep you.

May God bless you and
Increase in you the gift of love:
Constant love that is patient and kind,
Healing love that forgives and reconciles,
Attentive love that puts others first,
Enriching love that overflows to all around you,
Love that bears and hopes all things,
A love that endures and never ends.

May the blessings of God,
In you and upon you,
Keep you in perfect peace;
And by God's grace may
Your heart be content,
Let your hopes be fulfilled,
And your joy be complete.

Many the gifts of God to you:

Often the laughter, much the joy,

Little the sadness, short the trouble,

Long the friendships, deep the trust,

Infinitely great the love of God,

Eternal his blessings upon you.

Now and always, God bless you,

In sickness and in health, God be with you,

Coming in and going out, God watch over you,

Outwardly and inwardly, God guide you,

Lost and found, God embrace you,

Enough and overflowing, God give you love.

Over your waking and going out

Let God keep watch and guard you.

In your making and your working

Various gifts of God equip you.

Every night God bless your coming in.

Pour your love into Philip's heart,

Heavenly Father, God of love;

Invincible love, stronger than death,

Love which hopes and bears all things.

In your love without end bless him,

Protect him and keep him forever.

Pour your love into Phillipa's heart,

Heavenly Father, God of love;

Invincible love, stronger than death,

Love which hopes and bears all things,

Love which never comes to an end.

In your constant love bless her,

Provide for her, guide her,

And keep her always in your protection.

Respond with compassion to Rachael, Lord,

Answer with love her calling to you,

Come alongside her when she is lonely,

Hold her when she is sad.

And in her thinking and her speaking,

Everywhere she goes and everything she does,

Let your blessing be always upon her.

Richer may you be through the gifts of God,

In service more willing by his grace,

Clearer in your vision through the wisdom of God,

Kinder may you be in his love,

Your life be fuller with his blessings.

Rain softly, nurturing Lord,

On the soil of Rosie's nature;

Shine warmly, that she may grow

In your strength and flower in your beauty,

Every season of her life.

Second by second God bless you,

And hour by hour God support you,

Night by night God give you rest,

Day by day God give you hope,

Year after year God keep you in his love.

Send your blessings like sunshine, Lord,

And like rain upon the ground of Savannah's soul;

Vast be the horizons open before her,

And wider still your love to encompass her;

Numerous the flowers and fruits she bears,

Numberless the gifts you sow in her,

And deep her roots in the soil of your peace.

Speak, Lord, to your servant Simone,

In intimations of guidance and glory;

May she hear your still, small voice

Over the earthquake, wind and fire,

Narrating the story of your love,

Expressing your blessings upon her.

Shepherd God, guide Sofia,

Omniscient God, grant her wisdom,

Father God, keep her safe,

Inspirational God, be the creativity within her,

Almighty God, fill her with your love.

Shepherd God, guide Sophia,

Omniscient God, grant her wisdom,

Protector God, keep her safe,

Healing God, give her wholeness and health,

Inspirational God, be the creativity within her,

Almighty God, fill her with your love.

Set a garland of grace on Stefan, Lord;

Tailor a wardrobe of blessings for him,

Each garment bespoke and unique,

Fashioned from the fabric of peace,

And every stitch sewn by your hand, O Lord,

Neat with your care and strong with your love.

Set a garland of grace on Stephanie's head;

Tailor a garment of blessings for her,

Embroidered with joy on a fabric of peace;

Place it round her shoulders, Lord,

Her cloak of defence against all evil,

A robe whose stitches you sewed yourself,

Neat with your care and strong with your love,

In design uniquely shaped to her soul,

Exquisite in its beauty.

Set a garland of grace on Steve, Lord;

Tailor a wardrobe of blessings for him,

Each garment bespoke and unique,

Vestments fashioned from the fabric of peace,

Every stitch sewn with your love.

Since before your life began

Until the end of time itself,

Evermore may God bless you.

Traces of glory colour your vision,

Rumours of God whisper in your ear,

Aromas of God perfume your thinking.

Chords of heaven linger in your silences,

Echoes of the divine resonate in your speaking,

Your fabric of life be shot through with blessings.

Zealously may God keep you;

Abundantly may God bless you;

Constantly may God love you.

Zealous God, search and find you;

Almighty God, keep and protect you;

Kindly God, love and bless you.

INDEX

Names are listed alphabetically, with names in the appendix in italics. When looking for a name which appears in the appendix, please see the associated name in the main text (listed above it in the index) for an introduction and brief explanation of its meaning.

Aaron 2
Abigail 2
Abbie 227
Abby 227
Adam 3
Addison 3
Adrian 4
Agnes 4
Aidan 5
Aiden 227
Ailsa 5
Aimee 13
Alan 6
Allan 230
Alastair 6
Alasdair 228
Alistair 228
Albert 7
Alexander 7
Alex 8
Alexa 228
Alexandra 229
Alexis 229
Alfie 8
Alice 9
Alicia 229
Alisha 230
Alison 9
Allison 230
Allan 230 see Alan
Alyssa 10
Amalie 10

Amanda 11
Amber 12
Amelia 12
Amelie 231
Amy 13
Andrew 13
Andrea 231
Angela 14
Angel 231
Angelina 232
Angus 14
Ann 15
Anna 15
Annabel 15
Anne 232
Annette 232
Anthony 16
Anton 233
Antonia 233
Antonio 233
Antony 234
Archie 16
Ariana 17
Arianna 234
Arthur 17
Ashley 19
Ashton 19
Audrey 20
Austin 20
Ava 21
Bailey 21
Barbara 22

Barnaby 22
Beatrice 23
Belinda 23
Ben 24
Benjamin 24
Bethany 25
Betty 61
Beverley 25
Beverly 234
Billy 222
Billie 235
Blake 26
Bradley 26
Brandon 27
Brenda 27
Brendan 28
Brian 28
Brianna 235
Bryan 235
Bridget 29
Bronwen 29
Bronwyn 236
Brook 30
Brooke 30
Brooklyn 30
Bryan see Brian
Bryony 31
Briony 236
Caitlin 31
Caleb 33
Callum 33
Cameron 34

Camilla 34
Cara 35
Carla 35
Carly 236
Carole 36
Caroline 36
Carol 237
Carolyn 237
Catherine 37
Celia 37
Charles 38
Charlie 237
Charlotte 38
Chelsea 39
Cheryl 40
Chloe 40
Christian 41
Christine 42
Christina 238
Christopher 43
Clare 44
Claire 238
Clara 238
Colette 44
Cole 239
Colin 45
Connor 45
Cooper 46
Corey 46
Courtney 47
Craig 47
Crispin 48
Daisy 48
Daniel 49
Danielle 49
Daniella 239
Darren 50
David 50
Debbie 51
Deborah 51
Debra 239
Denis 52
Denise 52
Dennis 52

Derek 53
Destiny 53
Diana 54
Diane 54
Dominic 54
Don 55
Donald 55
Dorothy 55
Douglas 56
Dudley 56
Duncan 57
Dylan 57
Edward 58
Eileen 58
Elaine 59
Eleanor 59
Elijah 60
Elizabeth 61
Eliza 240
Ella 62
Ellie 62
Elliot 62
Eliott 240
Elliott 240
Ellis 63
Emilia 63
Emily 63
Emma 64
Eoghan 64
Eric 65
Erin 65
Ernest 66
Esme 66
Ethan 67
Evan 67
Eve 69
Eva 241
Evie 241
Evelyn 69
Ewan 69
Faith 70
Felicity 70
Findlay 71
Finlay 241

Finley 241
Finn 71
Fiona 72
Florence 72
Francesca 73
Francis 73
Frances 242
Frank 74
Freddie 74
Frederick 75
Freya 75
Gabriel 76
Gabriella 76
Gabrielle 242
Gail 77
Gareth 77
Gary 78
Gavin 78
Gemma 79
Geoff 79
Geoffrey 79
George 80
Georgia 243
Georgina 243
Gerald 80
Geraldine 244
Gerry 81
Gillian 81
Gill 244
Glyn 82
Glynn 82
Gordon 82
Grace 83
Gracie 244
Graham 83
Gwendoline 84
Gwen 245
Gwyneth 85
Gwynneth 85
Haley see Hayley
Hailey see Hayley
Hamish 85
Hannah 87
Harley 87

Harriet 88
Harrison 88
Harry 89
Harvey 89
Hayden 90
Hayley 90
  Haley 245
  Hailey 245
Heather 91
Heidi 91
Helen 92
  Helena 245
  Helene 245
Henry 92
  Henrietta 247
Hermione 93
Hilary 93
Holly 94
  Hollie 247
Howard 94
Hunter 95
Iain 95
Ian 95
Imogen 96
Irene 96
Isaac 97
Isabelle 97
  Isabel 248
  Isabella 248
Isaiah 98
Isla 99
Isobel 98
Jack 99
  Jackson 248
Jacob 100
Jacqueline 100
Jaden – see Jayden
Jake 101
James 101
Jamie 101
Jane 102
  Jayne 250
Janette 102
  Jan 249

Janet 249
Janine 249
Janice 102
Jasmine 103
Jason 103
Jay 104
Jayden 104
  Jaden 249
Jayne – see Jane
Jean 104
Jeffrey 105
Jemima 105
Jennifer 106
  Jenna 250
  Jennie 250
  Jenny 251
Jeremiah 106
Jeremy 107
Jerry 107
Jesse 108
Jessica 108
  Jessie 251
Jill 109
Joan 109
Joanna 109
  Joanne 251
Joe 113
Joel 110
John 110
Jonathan 111
Jordan 111
José 113
Joseph 113
Joshua 114
Joy 114
Joyce 115
Judith 115
  Judy 252
Julia 116
  Julian 252
  Julie 252
  Juliet 253
Juliette 116
Justin 117

Justine 117
Kai 117
Kaitlin 118
  Katelyn 253
Karen 118
Katherine 119
  Katharine 254
  Kathryn 254
Kathleen 121
Katie 120
Katrina 121
Kayla 123
  Kaylee 255
Kayleigh 123
Keira 124
Keith 124
Kelly 124
Kenneth 125
Kevin 125
Kian 126
Kieran 126
  Kieron 255
Kimberley 127
  Kimberly 255
Kirsty 127
Kitty 120
Kylie 128
  Kyle 256
Lacey 128
Lachlan 129
Lara 129
Laura 130
  Lauren 256
  Laurence 256
  Laurie 257
Lawrence 130
  Lawrie 257
Layla 131
Leah 131
Lee 131
Leo 132
  Leon 257
Lesley 132
Leslie 132

Lewis 133
Lexie 133
Lexi 257
Liam 133
Libby 134
Lily 134
Lillian 258
Lilly 258
Linda 134
Lynda 259
Lindsay 135
Lyndsay 259
Lindsey 135
Lisa 136
Logan 136
Lola 136
Lorna 137
Lorraine 137
Lottie 39
Louie 138
Louis 138
Louisa 138
Louise 138
Lucas 139
Luca 258
Lucinda 139
Lucy 139
Luis 138
Luisa 138
Luke 140
Lydia 140
Lyn 141
Lynda – see Linda
Lyndsay – see
  Lindsay
Lynn 141
Lynne 141
Lysbeth 141
Mackenzie 142
Maddison 142
Madison 259
Madeleine 143
Madeline 143
Maia – see Maya

Mair – see Mary
Maisie 143
Makayla 144
Michaela 263
Mikayla 263
Mala 144
Malcolm 145
Mandy 11
Marcus 145
Marcia 260
Margaret 146
Margery 261
Maria 147
Mariah 261
Marian 261
Marianne 262
Marie 262
Marilyn 147
Marion 262
Marjorie 146
Mark 148
Martha 148
Martin 149
Mary 149
Mair 260
Maryam 263
Mason 150
Matilda 150
Matthew 151
Maureen 151
Max 152
Maxwell 152
May 152
Maya 153
Maia 260
Megan 153
Melanie 155
Melissa 155
Mia 156
Michael 156
Michaela 263
Michelle 157
Mikayla 263
Millie 157

Molly 158
Mollie 264
Monica 158
Morgan 159
Muireann 159
Muriel 160
Nancy 160
Natalie 161
Natasha 161
Nathan 162
Nathaniel 162
Neil 163
Nevaeh 163
Neve 164
Niamh 164
Nicholas 165
Nicola 165
Nicole 264
Nigel 166
Nina 166
Noah 167
Norma 167
Norman 167
Oliver 169
Olivia 169
Olive 264
Oscar 170
Owen 170
Paige 170
Pamela 171
Pat 172
Patricia 171
Patrick 172
Paul 173
Paula 173
Pauline 173
Penny 174
Peter 174
Phillip 175
Philip 265
Philippa 175
Phillipa 265
Phoebe 176
Phyllis 176

Poppy 177
Quentin 177
Rachel 179
  Rachael 265
Ralph 179
Raymond 180
Rebecca 180
Reece 181
Reuben 181
Rhiannon 182
Rhys 182
Richard 183
  Ricky 266
Riley 183
Robert 184
Robin 184
Roger 185
Rory 185
Rose 186
  Rosie 266
Rosemary 186
Rowan 187
Rowena 187
Roy 188
Ruby 188
Ruth 188
Ryan 189
Sabine 189
Sally 189
Sam 191
Samantha 190
Samuel 190
Sandra 191
  Sandy 266
Sara 192
Sarah 192
Sasha 192

Savannah 193
  Savanna 267
Scarlett 193
Scott 194
Sean 194
Sebastian 195
Selina 195
Sharon 196
Sheila 196
Shirley 197
Siân 197
Siena 198
Sienna 198
Simon 198
  Simone 267
Simeon 199
Sinead 199
Skye 200
Sophie 200
  Sofia 267
  Sophia 268
Stanley 201
Stella 201
Stephen 202
  Stefan 268
  Stephanie 268
  Steve 269
Steven 202
Stewart 203
Stuart 203
Summer 204
Susan 205
  Sue 269
Suzanne 205
Sydney 206
Sylvia 206
Taylor 207

Teresa 207
Terry 208
Theo 208
Thomas 209
Tia 210
Tilly 210
Timothy 211
Toby 211
Tom 209
Tracy 213
  Tracey 269
Trevor 213
Trinity 214
Tyler 214
Una 215
Ursula 215
Valeria 217
Valerie 217
Vanessa 217
Vera 218
Veronica 218
Vicky 219
Victoria 219
Virginia 220
Wayne 220
Wendy 221
William 221
Willow 222
Xander 223
Xavier 223
Yvonne 225
Zachary 225
  Zac 269
  Zak 270
Zara 226
Zoe 226